ESSENTIALS OF

Conversation Analysis

Essentials of Qualitative Methods Series

ESSENTIALS OF

Conversation Analysis

Alexa Hepburn
Jonathan Potter

 AMERICAN PSYCHOLOGICAL ASSOCIATION

Published by
American Psychological Association
750 First Street, NE
Washington, DC 20002
https://www.apa.org

Order Department
https://www.apa.org/pubs/books
order@apa.org

In the U.K., Europe, Africa, and the Middle East, copies may be ordered from Eurospan
https://www.eurospanbookstore.com/apa
info@eurospangroup.com

Typeset in Charter and Interstate by Circle Graphics, Inc., Reisterstown, MD

Printer: Gasch Printing, Odenton, MD
Cover Designer: Anne C. Kerns, Anne Likes Red, Inc., Silver Spring, MD

Library of Congress Cataloging-in-Publication Data

Names: Hepburn, Alexa, author. | Potter, Jonathan, 1956- author.
Title: Essentials of conversation analysis / [Alexa Hepburn, Jonathan Potter].
Description: Washington, DC : American Psychological Association, [2021] |
   Series: Essentials of qualitative methods series | Includes bibliographical
   references and index.
Identifiers: LCCN 2021005924 (print) | LCCN 2021005925 (ebook) |
   ISBN 9781433835667 (paperback) | ISBN 9781433835698 (ebook)
Subjects: LCSH: Conversation analysis.
Classification: LCC P95.45 .H47 2021 (print) | LCC P95.45 (ebook) |
   DDC 302.34/6—dc23
LC record available at https://lccn.loc.gov/2021005924
LC ebook record available at https://lccn.loc.gov/2021005925

https://doi.org/10.1037/0000251-000

Printed in the United States of America

10 9 8 7 6 5 4 3 2 1

Contents

Series Foreword

Qualitative approaches have become accepted and indeed embraced as empirical methods within the social sciences, as scholars have realized that many of the phenomena in which we are interested are complex and require deep inner reflection and equally penetrating examination. Quantitative approaches often cannot capture such phenomena well through their standard methods (e.g., self-report measures), so qualitative designs using interviews and other in-depth data-gathering procedures offer exciting, nimble, and useful research approaches.

Indeed, the number and variety of qualitative approaches that have been developed is remarkable. We remember Bill Stiles saying (quoting Chairman Mao) at one meeting about methods, "Let a hundred flowers bloom," indicating that there are many appropriate methods for addressing research questions. In this series, we celebrate this diversity (hence, the cover design of flowers).

The question for many of us, though, has been how to decide among approaches and how to learn the different methods. Many prior descriptions of the various qualitative methods have not provided clear enough descriptions of the methods, making it difficult for novice researchers to learn how to use them. Thus, those interested in learning about and pursuing qualitative research need crisp and thorough descriptions of these approaches, with lots of examples to illustrate the method so that readers can grasp how to use the methods.

The purpose of this series of books, then, is to present a range of qualitative approaches that seemed most exciting and illustrative of the range of methods appropriate for social science research. We asked leading experts in qualitative methods to contribute to the series, and we were delighted that they accepted our invitation. Through this series, readers have the opportunity to learn qualitative research methods from those who developed the methods and/or who have been using them successfully for years.

We asked the authors of each book to provide context for the method, including a rationale, situating the method within the qualitative tradition, describing the method's philosophical and epistemological background, and noting the key features of the method. We then asked them to describe in detail the steps of the method, including the research team, sampling, biases and expectations, data collection, data analysis, and variations on the method. We also asked authors to provide tips for the research process and for writing a manuscript emerging from a study that used the method. Finally, we asked authors to reflect on the methodological integrity of the approach, along with the benefits and limitations of the particular method.

This series of books can be used in several different ways. Instructors teaching courses in qualitative research could use the whole series, presenting one method at a time to expose students to a range of qualitative methods. Alternatively, instructors could choose to focus on just a few approaches, as depicted in specific books, supplementing the books with examples from studies that have been published using the approaches, and providing experiential exercises to help students get started using the approaches.

In this book, Hepburn and Potter describe a challenging but rewarding approach to understanding everyday and organizational interactions. Their approach reveals how words are combined with tone, gesture, and setting to capture how people communicate. The authors provide a systematic method for analyzing spoken interaction that relies on close observation of actual communicative occasions rather than interviewing participants for their understanding of events, much as is done in other qualitative methods. The data generated are precise and reproducible rather than relying on interpretations by researchers. Although different structurally and philosophically from the other qualitative methods in this series, this method allows for a deep understanding of communication strategies and is applicable across many disciplines.

—*Clara E. Hill and Sarah Knox*

ESSENTIALS OF
Conversation Analysis

1 CONCEPTUAL FOUNDATIONS OF CONVERSATION ANALYSIS

Conversation analysis (CA) is a method for studying social life as it happens, in all its rich, varied, and intricate complexity. With over 50 years of development, it has revealed much about the basic architecture of social interaction and social life more broadly. CA has built a sophisticated understanding of practices in the kinds of everyday conversation that go on in phone calls, family dinners, or student dorms. This work has been developed to study interaction in professional or institutional settings: primary care consultations, helplines, psychotherapy and counseling, mediation, classroom interaction, news interviews, business meetings, legal settings. CA is a science based on direct observation of natural interaction that is not staged by the researcher; unlike much of the psychological mainstream, it uses neither experiments nor qualitative interviews to come to its conclusions. It reveals the basic ways in which speakers coordinate their talk; how they manage problems of production and understanding; how they perform offers and requests, complaints, and compliments; how they tell stories and indicate what they know and do not know; how emotion is displayed and responded to; how gaze, prosody, and gesture help to orchestrate interaction; and many more

https://doi.org/10.1037/0000251-001
Essentials of Conversation Analysis, by A. Hepburn and J. Potter

themes. These basic practices are refined and put to work in professional and institutional settings; CA reveals how each has a distinct architecture of interaction.

After over 50 years of progress, CA now boasts an international community of practitioners across sociology, linguistics, communication, anthropology, and psychology. Its main conference draws more than 500 attendees, and its literature is large and growing. CA aspires to a high level of scientific rigor in the production of precise and reproducible findings, and it has supported applied interventions, guided by its careful explication of how institutional interaction works and how professionals conduct their business. Although not developed specifically as an approach to psychology, contemporary CA reveals in extraordinary detail what it is to be human in any particular setting and throws important light on basic issues of knowledge and understanding, emotion and influence, intersubjectivity and intention, attitudes and beliefs, counseling and psychotherapy, and disability. The goal of this book is to introduce the method of CA. Compared with other approaches, a high proportion of research time is focused directly on analysis; high-quality analysis is what allows research to move forward. Our aim is to show what is involved in high-quality CA research. We begin this chapter with an illustration of how conversation analysts approach data and then consider the contextual and philosophical foundations of CA.

RATIONALE

Mum and Anna (her 3-year-old daughter) are British English speakers. The following fragment is from their midday meal. The notation used in the fragment is described in detail in Chapter 3. The lunch has been good-natured and chatty. Anna has eaten some, but not all, of her beans.

Extract 1.1. Eat Some Beans

```
01 Mum:    pt You still got some ↑bea:ns left ↑'aven't you:.
02         (2.7)
03 Anna:   Don' wan::ta bea::ns:
04         (0.5)
05 Mum:    You've to eat some bea:ns.
06         (1.2)
07 Anna:   °↓#Mm:,
08         (2.3)
09 Anna:   ((eats a spoonful then drops spoon on plate,
           lifts arms over head))
```

CA works with material like this. It is

- natural interaction made up of a series of turns of talk;

- recorded on digital video, allowing us to see what Mum and Anna can see: the beans on Anna's plate and Anna's gesture after eating the spoonful of beans;

- transcribed to capture features of delivery with added line numbers to allow us to point to specific features of the interaction (e.g., delay and pronunciation, changes in intonation and volume) because this is what people attend to when they are interacting with one another; and

- real life unfolding before us as researchers, laid out to capture most precisely how it unfolded for participants, which is most important. For conversation analysts, this kind of direct interaction between speakers is the primordial site of human social life.

Neither we, as researchers, nor Anna and Mum have functional magnetic resonance imaging recordings of brain states; nor have Anna and Mum been interviewed about what is going on or filled in survey questionnaires. Nevertheless, they talk in a coordinated way with one another, and that coordination is our focus. But where shall we look? If we focus just on grammar and abstract semantics, we might think that "You still got some ↑bea:ns left ↑'aven't you:." is merely presenting something Mum has noticed for confirmation with "↑'aven't you:.". Yet, at this point in the meal, the words "still" and "left" invoke a potential eating shortfall on Anna's part, perhaps indicating that there is still (healthy) eating to be done.

But the key thing that shows the coordination is that Anna's refusal on Line 03 treats what Mum is doing as requesting she eat her beans, albeit indirectly. Mum is performing an action, and building that action as simply noticing a shortfall is designed to allow Anna's possible resumption of eating to be relatively unforced. Anna's "Don' wan::ta bea::ns:" is pushing back against that action—she refuses the request. This pushback shows us as analysts what Anna's understanding is. Extract 1.1 also shows us that young children like Anna have already figured out that they need to tune into what the talk is doing—speakers do not simply focus on content; they focus on its action.

Conversation analysts work closely with participants' understandings of what is going on as those understandings unfold and change moment by moment in real time. But conversation analysts do not ask them about those understandings; rather, they study them in situ as displayed by participants, for participants in the turn-by-turn unfolding of their talk. The focus on what is displayed and the recipient's uptake provides a powerful check on analytic interpretation. For CA researchers, the response to a speaker's turn provides an important check on analytic interpretation; they refer to this as the next turn proof procedure (Sacks et al., 1974). Any speaker's analysis of the prior turn's action is relevant to their construction of their own next turn, so it is their analysis that conversation analysts seek to represent. Note that it is a radically different approach from more common alternatives that tend to work through questioning people about their understandings (or views, beliefs, feelings, and so on) post hoc. These understandings are then typically seen as lying below the "surface" of talk, requiring special research instruments to access. For us, the medium of talk provides its own system for understanding, and much of the important business of psychology lives and works in that system.

Conversation analysts focus on the actions performed in interaction—and they have this focus because that is the focus of our participants. Actions are mostly done through talk, and thus CA is sometimes called the study of talk-in-interaction, to acknowledge that interaction is not simply talk. In its early years, CA researchers typically used recordings of interactions on the phone as data (e.g., Schegloff & Sacks, 1973). This has the analytic virtue that participants cannot see facial expressions and movement, thus simplifying the focus of analysis. Moreover, a traditional telephone call is limited to two parties. However, as researchers have focused increasingly on records of copresent interaction, and now interaction mediated through screens such as those of Zoom or Skype, they have addressed issues of embodied (sometimes referred to as "multimodal") action and the way gaze, gesture, and bodily orientation are coordinated with talk to contribute to ongoing actions. In this case, for example, Mum's initial reference to beans is bright and cheerful—the arrows in the transcript mark upward intonation. And she is simultaneously looking away from Anna and emptying a packet of potato chips onto her own plate. The project of getting Anna to eat her beans is done lightly here—almost as a reminder. Later in the extract, we can see how Anna shows that she has completed the bean-eating project by dropping her spoon and putting her hands above her head; she literally embodies it. We have seen that Mum's "You still got some ↑bea:ns left ↑'aven't you:." is a kind of request. Typically, in conversation, actions come in pairs—question and answer, greeting and greeting, complaint and apology, and so on. The technical term for such pairs of actions is *adjacency pairs*. For now, note that a request like this sets up a limited set of response possibilities. Anna could comply with the request, finishing off her beans; she could decline, maybe with an account—she is full up or does not like them. Alternatively, she could try to ignore the request altogether, or maybe she could do something that makes it unclear whether she is going to comply or decline—we might call that *incipient compliance*. This range of options highlights two things. First, in natural interaction, actions are not caused by one another; rather, their relations are contingent. If parental requests simply and directly caused children's compliance, family life would be a somewhat alarming world of mechanical order and discipline. Instead, we see a different form of order, showing actions and different kinds of possible resistance. Second, this contingency is not random or infinite. An action sets up an orderly set of response possibilities (and these response possibilities in turn set up an orderly set of further response possibilities). CA studies the systematic organization of contingent action.

The fact that conversational actions have these systematic options means they exist as a powerful inferential system for participants. Mum's expectation is that the next action will come from a limited set of options. The issuing of an action outside of these limited possibilities is not impossible, but it may lead Mum to think that she has misheard or Anna has misspoken. Conversation analysts have, in fact, documented an intricate set of possible repair operations directed at fixing problems with talk, which we discuss in Chapter 5. However, the power of CA is that actual interaction is studied. Here we have Anna's actual response to Mum's request. This is more analytically powerful than speculating about what might have happened.

We have discussed just a brief fragment to illustrate key issues. Actions are threaded together in sequences, and those sequences are themselves organized in systematic ways that conversation analysts have documented (Schegloff, 2007b). In Extract 1.1, for example, Mum responds to Anna's pushback by upgrading from a request to a more explicit directive on Line 05: "You've to <u>e</u>at some <u>b</u>ea:ns.". This patterning, where parental projects of behavior modification become increasingly insistent, is regularly found in parent–child interaction sequences and give us a way to address broader questions about socialization (Hepburn, 2020). The organization of sequences is a major concern for speakers, and that makes it a major tool for conversation analysts.

The fact that interaction is intrinsically contingent means that turns can be designed in very different ways. We have seen how the request in Line 01 is indirect; rather than using a standard grammatical request form, it is formulated as a *noticing*. It could have drawn on different words (different lexical items) or different grammar, used different prosody (varying stress and intonation), and so on. These possibilities are important for the different expectations they set up. They work to shape what comes next. *Action formation* is, therefore, another major field of CA research. Conversation analysts study how turns are put together to accomplish actions. One way of thinking of this is that the aim of CA is to reveal how the machinery of interaction works.

Our illustrative example focused on everyday interaction in a family setting. As we noted at the outset, CA research on everyday talk has provided a platform for the systematic understanding of how interaction works in professional and institutional settings. Often, this shows how everyday conversational forms are refined or exploited in the institutional setting (Drew & Heritage, 1992). For example, in a children's bullying helpline, advice may be embedded in questions ("Have you talked to a teacher?"; Butler et al., 2010); television news interviewers often build challenging questions by embedding them in the views of "experts" or "political opponents" (Heritage & Clayman, 2010). CA provides a powerful set of tools for understanding what happens in institutions. Knowing the specific ways in which interaction is organized in an institution can, for example,

- help us to recruit more participants into mediation (by building rejection of mediation as being "unwilling" to participate; Sikveland & Stokoe, 2016),

- keep critical callers on the line in 911 calls (by highlighting the impending transfer to dispatch for more information just when the caller completes their report and may expect to close; Kevoe-Feldman & Pomerantz, 2018), and

- limit unnecessary antibiotic prescription (through the clinician's "on-line commentary" during the diagnostic phase of the visit; Heritage & Stivers, 1999).

Interest in institutional problems often brings researchers into CA, but that work is supported by continuing development in the study of everyday talk.

HISTORICAL AND THEORETICAL ORIGINS

CA was developed throughout the 1960s and 1970s by the sociologist Harvey Sacks, who was influenced by Harold Garfinkel (the founder of ethnomethodology), as well as by the sociologist Erving Goffman. Sacks worked originally with Emmanuel Schegloff and Gail Jefferson. The key publication that did much to establish the power and ambition of CA was a paper by Sacks and colleagues (1974) on the systematics that underpin conversation. This went on to become one of the most influential papers in the history of social science—and has accrued nearly 20,000 citations across a wide spread of disciplines. Soon after its publication, Sacks was killed in a car crash. His influence lives on not just through his relatively small number of publications but also through his lectures at the University of California Irvine delivered throughout the 1960s. These had been circulated informally around the CA community and were finally formally published in 1992. They provide an extraordinary insight into the intensity of his thinking and the range of his ideas; they still repay careful reading.

One way to think of CA is as a form of observational science. It is no accident that CA developed in tandem with developments of easily used mobile audio recorders and, more recently, cheap, portable digital video with the associated range of viewing and editing software. This enabled an approach to observation that is grounded in records that can be reviewed, edited, and reproduced, something not available to earlier social and psychological observational approaches that used field notes or checklists (e.g., Bales, 1950; Barker & Wright, 1951). CA can also be contrasted with the influential perspective on language developed by Noam Chomsky and, in particular, the claim that "performance" (i.e., natural conversation) data are too messy for researchers to work with because of their creative and almost infinitely open-ended nature (Chomsky, 2006). Chomsky's arguments discouraged a generation of cognitive psychologists from looking at conversation in its home settings. That is one reason why CA evolved outside of psychology and linguistics.

Taking a diametrically opposite approach to Chomsky, Sacks founded a scientific discipline that allowed researchers to record the mundane—phone calls among family members—or the challenging—police emergency calls, treatment decision making with breast cancer patients—and look inside the machinery that organizes interaction in these areas. He showed that performance data is certainly complicated, but it is far from messy—it has a flexible order that reflects the different projects and considerations that play out as humans join in interaction and as these contingencies act on one another. Crucially, Sacks showed that interaction can be studied in a rigorous and methodical fashion. In this book, we show how you can begin such a study.

CONVERSATION ANALYSIS AND THE QUALITATIVE TRADITION

One way to highlight the distinctive nature of CA methods is to think about the data with which it works. Overwhelmingly, CA works with audio and, where relevant, video recordings of interaction in either everyday or institutional settings, supplemented by precise transcription that captures features of delivery such as overlaps and delay, stress, prosody, and volume. These are *naturalistic data*, records of interaction not staged specifically for a researcher (Potter & Shaw, 2018). For example, the family seen in Extract 1.1 were lent a small portable video camera and asked to record around 15 mealtimes. This interaction would have happened whether the researcher was involved or not. The record is not structured or predefined by a researcher. What is collected is not a secondary report of events told to the researcher, nor a set of responses to a fixed-choice questionnaire or survey, nor the result of an experimental protocol. Naturalistic data of this kind allow the researcher to review the actions, events, and phenomena that are studied, returning to the original recordings for new analyses at any time.

Sacks (1992) expressed the methodological ideal in this way: "I am trying to develop [an analytic approach] where the reader has as much information as the author, and can reproduce the analysis" (p. 27). And he explicitly compared this with the methods section of a biology paper designed to allow any new researcher to reproduce the study. He wanted the researcher to be accountable to the data in a way that is direct and precise. If a phenomenon is being claimed, it must be demonstrated in the examples offered—it is not the product of commentary on something to be taken on trust, nor is it refined from an aggregate or statistical generalization. The claims need to work in each case and work together for the pattern claimed.

Although CA was not established specifically to counter quantitative traditions of social research, close analysis highlights challenging problems for any counting and coding done before a fully developed interaction analysis. Emmanuel Schegloff (1993) laid out some of the complexities in moving from close analysis of conversational practices to broader generalizations, let alone connecting those generalizations to classes of individuals.

The point is not that conversation analysts are against quantification in principle or aspire to be aligned with humanistic perspectives. Their analytic approach is designed to do justice to the various phenomena of conversation. As the body of conversational research has grown, and particular phenomena and practices have been clearly described, it has been possible to build studies that support broader numerical summaries or statistical generalizations. These are the exception, however, and high-quality CA is typically performed without extensive quantification and statistical analysis.

CA overlaps certain strands of discourse analysis, particularly the tradition developed out of Jonathan Potter and Margaret Wetherell's (1987) *Discourse and Social Psychology*, which drew heavily on CA and ethnomethodology. Although there are some tensions over questions of method and theory, the field of discursive psychology that emerged from this can be thought of as primarily the application of CA theory and method to distinctively psychological questions (Potter, 2021).

CA can also be contrasted with approaches that fall within the social constructionist tradition in sociology and psychology. These approaches tend to focus on individual construction—what people think or feel or how they tell stories to create their social worlds. Although not couched in the language of constructionism, CA does link to some constructionist themes. In particular, conversation analysts have considered the way descriptions are built to form a particular action (action formation will be covered in detail in Chapter 4). Consider the different descriptions of events in a rape trial from the defense counsel and the victim:

Extract 1.2

```
01 C:  And during the evening, didn't Mr. O [the defendant]
02     come over to sit with you?
03 W:  Sat at our table.
```

In his study of accusations in legal settings, Paul Drew (1992) focused on how actions are built in the legal cross-examination through constructing versions of events that provide for upshots and inferences. In Lines 01 to 02, the rapist's defense council's version implies a preexisting and perhaps close relationship "sit with you." The victim counters with a competing version that undermines this version with its possibly damaging implications. In this specific but profound sense, CA is constructionist.

THE PHILOSOPHICAL AND EPISTEMOLOGICAL BACKGROUND TO CONVERSATION ANALYSIS

In Harvey Sacks's lectures, he references a wide range of sources from philosophy, sociology, anthropology, and psychology. But these were signposts and jumping-off points rather than foundations. Sacks's early work used recordings from a suicide counseling hotline and group therapy sessions. He was respectful of ethnographic writing (in both its sociological and anthropological traditions), emphasizing the direct engagement with life ethnography brings. As he put it, "I would treat it as the only work worth criticizing in sociology; where criticizing is giving some dignity to something" (Sacks, 1992, p. 27). Sacks was particularly critical of the way presumptive analytic claims can be baked into ethnographic field notes. For example, describing participants' actions and feelings is fixing a particular analytic judgment into the notes, and those judgments cannot be unpicked, looking back on the sequence of talk or prosodic nature of the delivery. CA's reliance on audio and video records, combined with rigorous transcription, is designed to counter this problem by grounding analysis more directly in records of action that can be continually reviewed.

Major influences on his work came from Erving Goffman (e.g., 1959) and Harold Garfinkel (1967), who were both involved in Sacks's PhD training. Goffman developed the idea that underlying the existing social institutions sociologists have studied there is a distinctive *interaction order*. This order is made up of a web of rights and obligations, a person's "face" in interaction, and is linked to issues of identity. This provides for the public accountability of a person's actions and related issues of motive and identity. CA was built to offer a more empirically grounded and systematic approach to the sets of issues that Goffman highlighted (Schegloff, 1988). But it retains his central insight that researchers can study an interaction order that is distinct from the classic institutions theorized by sociology.

Harold Garfinkel is most associated with the development of *ethno-methodology*—the study of members' commonsense methods for making sense of the world. In CA, the study of members' methods is developed in the distinct environment of conversation. For example, we might consider how the particle "huh?" is used by members as a method for showing that they have a problem with what has been just said that needs fixing or repair-ing and also showing that the speaker is not clear on precisely what kind of problem it is (e.g., mishearing, misunderstanding). In CA, this practice (or members' method) is called an *open-class repair initiator*, and it is one of a set of practices of repair (which we discuss in Chapter 5).

In the context of this book's focus on methods and psychology, it is important to emphasize that neither Goffman nor Garfinkel was developing psychological approaches to social life; rather, their concern was with its orderly coordination. Nor were they attempting to find psychological drivers for sociological phenomena. Garfinkel, in particular, claimed in early writing that there is nothing interesting under the skull. This anticognitivism appears in later ethnomethodological work. CA is typically more cautious or agnostic with respect to cognition (see papers in te Molder & Potter, 2005).

Sacks also engaged with themes from Ludwig Wittgenstein's later phi-losophy. In his best-known book, *Philosophical Investigations*, Wittgenstein (1953) rejected the picture of language as a formal, unitary system used for abstract reasoning and making reference to both mental and physical entities. Instead, he proposed that we think of language as a toolbox, with different tools specialized for different tasks. The familiar Wittgenstein aphorism is that "meaning is use." Rather than think of the meaning of a word as a conceptual entity found through a dictionary definition, look to how that word is used in a situated practice.

There are striking similarities between the formal structure of Sacks's lectures and Wittgenstein's (1953) *Philosophical Investigations*. Both engage with conversational fragments, teasing away at the practices they display. Both move away from mentalistic interpretations of notions such as knowing, seeing, or understanding. For example, conversation analysts see under-standing as something that is displayed in the very organization of talk; as one turn builds on and responds to the previous, it provides a public display of how the speaker has understood what has come before (Sacks et al., 1974, p. 728). The notion of display is central to interaction because sustaining coordination through joint projects, even antagonistic ones, requires an ongoing understanding of what the other is doing. When you respond to a compliment with an appreciation ("Well, thank you") or an injection of modesty ("It's just something I threw on"), you are simultaneously doing the work of appreciating or being modest and displaying that you have iden-tified what was said as a compliment. CA thus provides a profound and analytically grounded take on the notion of intersubjectivity by identifying practices that work to keep participants aligned with one another in inter-action (e.g., Schegloff, 1992). In this sense, Wittgenstein's and Sacks's conceptual insights overlap. However, Sacks moved beyond Wittgenstein's use of invented and imagined examples to focus exclusively on instances taken from natural interaction. This book is focused on showing how to analyze such material.

HOW TO READ THIS BOOK

The book is designed as a practical analytic handbook that provides a comprehensive introduction to the different elements and phases in analyzing conversation—something to have open next to you while you are working through a data set. As such, you may find it most useful to target particular chapters at different stages of your research. For researchers unfamiliar with CA, Chapter 1 will give you a general feel of the perspective, and Chap-ters 6 and 7 show how the method hangs together. Then you could select one or two papers from the exemplar studies list in the Appendix and read them carefully, thinking of the questions they raise for you. At this point, you might well quickly read the rest, with a focus on Chapters 4 and 5, which provide an overview of the key conversational areas that will help you into analysis. These two chapters contain relatively dense summaries of basic phenomena—they will come most alive for you as you use them to explore your own materials. As you move forward with an actual project, Chapter 2 will prepare you for data collection and issues of technology, data management, and recruiting participants. When you have collected data, you will want to work with Chapter 3, which is designed to support you in making high-quality transcripts. Note that we often italicize key technical terms, which will be unpacked at various points throughout the book.

This book will bring the most reward when you combine analysis and reading. As you come to write up the research, Chapter 6 will come into its own. As you will no doubt discover as you read through this volume, CA research has a distinct approach to interaction and a lot of technical tools to assist with analysis. We advise novice researchers to have someone on the supervisory team who has had CA training.

SUMMARY

CA focuses on actions and interactions. These actions are often organized into pairs, with one speaker producing an action and another producing a response or next action of some kind. These pairs are often expanded into sequences that have their own standardized organization. The turns of talk that speakers produce can be formed in different ways using different words, grammatical constructions, and so on to accomplish the action. As speakers interact, their turns of talk display their moment-by-moment ongoing understandings of what is going on; this keeps conversationalists coordinated with one another and is a key resource for analysts of conversation. The ongoing display of understanding provides conversationalists an immediate indication if something has gone wrong. If talk gets broken in some way, conversationalists can draw on an elaborate machinery to repair it; mistakes are common in conversation, but there is continual work to fix them and prevent the cumulative problems that would have arisen if they went unfixed. Although the core is interaction done through talk in everyday and institutional settings, CA provides a systematic way into the study of gesture and embodiment, the use of texts and displays in interaction, and various forms of "new media" communication.

2 DESIGNING AND CONDUCTING CONVERSATION ANALYSIS

In this chapter, we explore some of the most basic requirements for conducting a conversation analysis (CA) study: gaining access to research sites, collecting and managing data, generating a focus aided by existing literature, and formulating initial research questions to move forward with Jeffersonian transcription (Chapter 3).

GAINING ACCESS AND RECRUITING PARTICIPANTS

CA works exclusively with naturally occurring material from either everyday or institutional settings. Note the focus on settings rather than people—our aim is not to seek statistical representativeness of individuals in a population but rather to understand the core communicative practices within each setting (we write about identifying practices later). This means that research access is one of the fundamental challenges for doing high-quality research. With everyday interaction, this is relatively straightforward, although the individuals or families will need to be carefully briefed about what the recordings are to be used for and who will watch or listen to them,

https://doi.org/10.1037/0000251-002
Essentials of Conversation Analysis, by A. Hepburn and J. Potter

paying particular attention to any younger children. Participants are often recruited through networks of students and their families.

For institutional settings, careful negotiation may be required to help participants trust researchers, clarify how (non) invasive the work is, and show the value of the work. Choice of institutional research site will be dependent on the researcher's interests—how 911 calls are organized, say, or how counseling is delivered to callers to a helpline. In each case, we will need to work with the appropriate organization, their institutional review board processes, and perhaps their legal constraints.

CA researchers have had success negotiating access to even the most delicate contexts. This is often a result of developing a collaborative partnership with participants and demonstrating familiarity with the research site (Hepburn & Potter, 2004). Qualitative researchers commonly plead that it is too difficult to obtain records of naturally occurring data, and so they default to conducting interviews or surveys (see Potter & Hepburn, 2005, for problems with interview-based work). However, in our experience, permission can be gained for access to the most challenging settings if participants are approached carefully, the nature and scope of the research are carefully described, and trust is established.

The first approach to potential participants will likely cover a number of topics. First and foremost, because our work is fundamentally evidence based, it involves recording actual interaction. This means video as well as audio where speakers are copresent—sometimes more than one camera will be needed to capture facial expressions, gestures, and so forth. If participants are professionals in a work setting, they may be expecting you to ask them to fill in surveys about what they do or be interviewed rather than recorded, so attending to the following points up front can help to quell any fears people might have.

Practitioners' anxieties about performance can be tackled by noting that you are not trying to highlight individual quirks or insufficiencies. Rather, the focus will be on identifying generic practices of effective communication or widely experienced challenges across a corpus of anonymized extracts. It is extremely rare for CA work to highlight differences in conversational style between people. This focus tends to be more reassuring to practitioners and could still allow for interesting discussions with them about what might constitute less effective practices in any feedback sessions. Concerns that we often need to address up front include the following:

- Participation is voluntary and, at any stage, participants may ask to stop and delete the recording.

- The risk for any individual when participating is low.
- The equipment will be set up beforehand, so the researcher will not be present during the interaction.

Ethical requirements can be complex for this kind of research, but we now have some effective technological solutions that deliver high levels of anonymity:

- We can store data in such a manner that linkage between a participant's identity and the recordings and access to those unanonymized recordings can be made password dependent.

- Short extracts that we show to other researchers or practitioners can be anonymized by disguising voices and physical characteristics and blanking out person and place names or other identifying information.

In return for access, we can offer

- customized feedback, with a focus on things that practitioners want more support with (strategies for soothing strong emotion, say, or managing advice resistance);

- detailed engagement and high-level discussions about practitioners' work; and

- practitioners' involvement with the analytic process, where they prove invaluable in advisory group settings. Sometimes they may become coauthors on publications.

DATA COLLECTION

Collecting high-quality, naturally occurring data is a crucial first step. In CA, our focus is typically on practices within specific settings, which means we take a different approach to sampling than other researchers. If we are collecting institutional data, we look to capture a spread of examples—for example, from different call takers if we are looking at 911 calls or different therapists if we are looking at family therapy. Mostly we are searching for practices that appear across a corpus. Once a practice has been identified, we can look for it in new settings; we may need to adjust the goals of a study in the course of recruiting, consenting, and collecting data as we do this.

There are also more practical issues, such as placement of recording equipment, what to record, and when to record it. Decisions like these can involve subtle trade-offs—the following provides a guide (see Mondada, 2013, for more detail):

- Position recording equipment in such a way that you include all participants in the recording, whether audio or video.

- If you are working with video, do not be tempted to focus solely on "talking heads"—you may become particularly focused on the coordination of the interaction with the use of various objects, tools, screens, or body movements—for example, the complex concurrent activities within the operating room of a surgical department (Mondada, 2011).

- Think about how long you will need to record for (this can affect your choice of equipment), how much data storage is possible, and how far quality is reduced by compression of data. Once access has been granted and equipment is in place, there is value in collecting more material because this is relatively low effort and cost and can support unforeseen research developments and new projects.

- Sensitive settings may benefit from less obtrusive recording equipment, although there is a trade-off with recording quality—for example, if you have only one recorder, you may lose the facial expressions of one or more of the parties. Anything that impairs your ability to transcribe participants' conduct—for example, large groups talking together, situations with lots of background noise, or lack of adequate lighting—will make your data difficult to work with, less reliable, and much more time consuming.

Having gained access to a research site, it is important to seek insights into the participants and their roles—for example, what their typical work practices might be and who they are to one another (e.g., doctor–patient, close friends, mother–son). When analysis is underway, these initial understandings are likely to be refined.

RESEARCH TEAM CONSIDERATIONS

As you will no doubt discover as you read through this volume, CA research has a distinct approach to interaction and a lot of technical tools to assist with analysis. This makes it hard to simply start doing analysis on your own with only this short book as a guide. It will be useful to have someone on your team who has had CA training and has published in your general area of interest. That person will probably be involved in data sessions (see the following section), which are usually available to attendees, coresearchers, or graduate students. If it is not possible to have a CA researcher on your team, then attending local or remote data sessions becomes even more crucial (see the following section for suggestions).

There are further team considerations where interaction in non-English languages is involved. Our typical advice is that the primary researcher should be a native speaker of the language in which they are working. That researcher may well work alongside other researchers who are not native speakers. In data sessions, it is quite common to work with non-English materials and work with the original recording (ideally, with verbatim subtitles if it is video), native language transcript of that recording, and English language transcript.

DATA SESSIONS

Data sessions play an important part in developing analysis. CA researchers work in data sessions with other experienced analysts. A typical data session will involve playing of one or more recordings multiple times and sometimes begin with refining the transcript. Analytic observations will refer back to the transcript or the recording and often both. Even well-used transcripts by expert transcribers can be subject to improvement as new hearings, perhaps with better equipment or refined conventions, allow for minor changes. There is often a particular focus in data sessions on the transcription of those sections of recordings that will have a role in supporting research claims. When conducting data sessions with materials for the first time, the focus will often be a largely inductive exploration of anything interesting that emerges from the data. A productive data session will often focus on one segment of data and zero in on a single part of that segment. Later on, the analytic attention will focus on specific practices as observations about (often previously undiscovered) phenomena get refined.

There are many data sessions worldwide that welcome visitors and/or virtual participants. See https://rolsi.net/data-sessions/ for a list. There are also completely remote data sessions that you can join and bring your data—see https://sites.google.com/york.ac.uk/remotedatasessions/home for details. Saul Albert's blog (http://saulalbert.net/blog/how-to-prepare-for-an-emca-data-session/) is also full of useful advice about preparing for a data session. Another useful addition to the research team can be to have one or more of the practitioners whose data you are working with involved in helping you to make sense of the data—for example, if it contains technical jargon or complex decision making.

ADJUSTING FOR BIASES AND EXPECTATIONS

It may be useful to stop here and think about the difference between CA and most other forms of qualitative methods that rely on researchers interviewing participants themselves. It is usually the case with such techniques that one must train interviewers to facilitate interaction in such a way that allows participants' views to emerge rather than be influenced by the researcher. With CA this is one big problem that we do not have to think about (see Hepburn & Potter, 2004, for more elaboration). Analysts are supplied with the tools for documenting how participants make sense of one another. Nevertheless, one of the points of opening your data to scrutiny by other conversation analysts—for example, through your research team and via data sessions and ultimately peer review—is to ensure that you are staying true to participants' orientations to one another rather than describing aspects of the data that support whatever theories, ideas, or agendas to which you may be committed. For example, if you are analyzing police interviews, you may be predisposed to discount the victim's accounts and explanations or see the police questioning as overly invasive or accusatory.

As we see in Chapters 6 and 7, when you are publishing your analysis, there are further levels of checking for biases available. Papers in CA can often look data heavy, but this allows other researchers—readers and reviewers—to evaluate the claims you make and adjust them if needed. As Sacks (1984) put it, "Others could look at what I had studied and make of it what they could, if, for example, they wanted to be able to disagree with me" (p. 26). For this to happen, it is important to provide extracts that start at the beginning of a sequence (see Chapter 4) rather than partway through. This greatly contributes to the integrity of the analysis, discussed in more detail in Chapter 7.

RESEARCH QUESTIONS

It may seem odd to focus on research questions at this early stage before you begin transcribing. However, once you start to look at your naturally occurring interaction, it can seem incredibly complex, and as we see in Chapter 3, the work of Jeffersonian transcribing can be time-consuming, so it is often useful to approach your initial collection building with some broader questions in mind, allowing you to identify sequences that are likely to be worth the investment of time. More pragmatically, you may also be thinking of developing research proposals, where you will typically need to generate aims and objectives—answering clear research questions becomes a useful tool in doing this.

Research questions in CA can be something of a moving target due to the inductive nature of the work. At this early stage, you might explore something that encompasses a range of practices, such as "What is the interactional role of laughter?" This then focuses your data collection and data management into a broad corpus of examples. Only after analysis will it become clear how those questions can be refined and different studies developed (see early work by Jefferson, 1984, and studies in Glenn & Holt, 2013, for analyses of laughter in talk).

CA research questions are not focused on identifying presumed psychological phenomena lying behind talk; CA is focused on how people get things done in and through talk—including things that researchers might consider exclusively "psychological" (e.g., see Voutilainen et al., 2010). This means that rather than "What are providers' and patients' experiences of empathy?" we might ask, "What does empathy look like in medical consultations?" For this, we would need to ask, "What practices accompany turns that appear to display 'empathy'?" and "How do those practices play out?" (see Ford et al., 2019, for an example from palliative care hospice data, and Hepburn & Potter, 2007, for helpline research). To refine our research questions, we may turn to the CA literature and find, for example, that empathy has been written about in analysis of end-of-life discussions but less explored in the therapeutic context, and this might lead to further more specific questions about different empathic practices and their function across different contexts. It is inevitable that the preliminary questions will themselves be refined or even abandoned once full analysis gets underway. Often, viewing it in its interactional context encourages us to rethink the nature of the analytic object. Looking for empathy in a child protection helpline interaction, for example, can start to rework what it means to be empathic.

Most CA collections are of phenomena such as the following:

- a practice, such as starting a conversational turn with an "oh" preface or initial address term (explained further in the section titled Person Reference in Chapter 5) or responding to a directive;

- a social action, such as requesting, announcing news, complaining, apologizing, or complimenting;

- a specialized activity, such as advising callers on a helpline, delivering a diagnosis, or history taking in a medical consultation; or

- some hitherto unnoticed technical feature of social interaction, such as a new kind of other-initiated repair or preference organization (see Chapters 4 and 5).

The following are some more examples of broader research questions that you might start with:

- How are different interactional practices—for example, advising, soothing, information gathering, directing—designed and delivered within your data set?

- Relatedly, which of these communicative activities appears to be most effective in which environments, and what counts as effective to which parties in the interaction?

- How do participants manage interpersonal and institutional alignments?

- How do practitioners connect with each other, formally and informally, as part of doing their job?

- How do different institutional policies and training procedures compare with actual practices of interaction?

- How is emotion considered from an interactional perspective? (See the collections in Peräkylä & Sorjonen, 2012, and Ruusuvuori, 2013, for ideas on how researchers have tackled this.)

IDENTIFYING PRACTICES

CA studies may focus on specific social actions, such as requesting or complaining, or other activities, such as advising, that are fairly straight-forward to identify. Often, however, the focus is on describing practices and the actions they accomplish. By "practices," we mean specific features of the design of turns in conversation. Practices are context-free phenomena; we can use our understanding of their meaning to analyze new data and gain deeper insights into what speakers are doing. An example of a practice is using an *open class repair initiator* (e.g., Huh? Sorry? What?). However, practices are also context sensitive, meaning they can be exploited in different ways in different contexts to perform specific tasks. For example, in some contexts, "What?" might simply indicate a problem in hearing the prior turn; in others, the speaker may hear perfectly well what was said but display that it was problematic or inapposite in some way (Drew, 1997). Hence, although open class repair initiators typically give the opportunity to say something more clearly, on occasion, they can be used to imply that the speaker is mistaken or confused (Robinson, 2006).

The focus on practices plays a major role in how CA researchers refine their questions, often starting with more vernacular notions and then providing a more technical specification of what is going on (see Chapters 4 and 5, where we go through the steps of conducting a CA). To illustrate using a different example, we might be interested in the following research question: "What is the function of a *turn-initial address term* used for a copresent speaker?"—thus, "Helen, we've been through this," where "Helen" is the turn-initial address term (see Chapter 5, Person Reference, for explication). Why use the kind of reference term that normally comes at the start of an interaction when it is obvious to all parties to whom the speaker is talking? Using a turn-initial address turn is one practice we could study, and our focus would be on the actions it accomplishes—what speakers are doing with it (see Clayman, 2010, for an example).

Practices may also occur sequentially. For example, CA researchers might be interested in the way children respond to parents' directing actions and then start to explore how parents manage resistance to their directives. We address these questions by making collections of a practice and conducting analysis to explicate their pattern. For example, directive actions regularly lead to one of two responses: The recipient complies or defies. However, directives may also be ignored, and sometimes a response is deferred (Craven & Potter, 2010). Directive actions can be designed to achieve a specific response. To illustrate, in the previous chapter we discussed the following example:

Extract 2.1. Crouch 08 8.36

```
01 Mum:    pt You still got some ↑bea:ns left ↑'aven't you:.
02         (2.7)
03 Anna:   Don' wan::ta bea::ns:
04         (0.5)
05 Mum:    You've to eat some bea:ns.
06         (1.2)
07 Anna:   °↓#Mm:,
08         (2.3)
09 Anna:   ((eats a spoonful then drops spoon on plate, lifts
           arms over head))
```

We noted how Anna treats Mum's turn on Line 01 as a request to eat her beans—and so something that she has the choice of refusing on Line 03. Mum then reformulates her turn on Line 05 more overtly: "You've to eat some bea:ns." This is a common pattern that we find in directive sequences of talk—that the speaker begins by requesting or simply noticing something awry. We can now pick out some interesting elements about Anna's responsive turns: First, they are delayed—note the 1- and 2-second silences on Lines 06 and 08. Then there is a quietly delivered protest sound on Line 07, followed by compliance on Line 09. Note that for Anna, compliance consists of eating a single spoonful of beans, and the sequence continues with Mum's attempts to have her eat more. Parent–child interaction is made up of multitudes of conversational practices; CA researchers start to document the specifics of their operation in concrete settings, with a broader aim of revealing the patterning of these practices (e.g., how they operate in "socialization"; Hepburn, 2020).

We started with a research question focused on a particular sequential practice related to how children respond to parents' directive actions. However, such is the richness of this type of data that even this short clip can stimulate numerous further research questions. For example, "How do parents get their children to eat healthy food?" or "What strategies do parents have for dealing with children's resistance to directive actions?" or "Why use a noticing rather than a request?" These broader questions might be a pathway to the identification of further conversational practices and actions across our data.

Once we have identified a focus and generated research questions that allow us to build a collection and analyze it, we then have a useful resource for future analysis. For example, understanding the range of ways one can build up to a directive or an admonishing action might allow one to make greater sense of sequences that end in more severe parent–child conflict. This is no small thing; it could allow us to improve training in basic parenting skills. And yet, we are barely even at the foothills of understanding the range of practices that make up conversation. This work takes time and effort to do well, but the payoff is that we can gain new and exciting insights into human life. Most CA researchers have a deep fascination with charting previously unidentified human practices as they unfold.

BUILDING COLLECTIONS AND MANAGING DATA

Collecting, transcribing, and analyzing go hand in hand. When you start to build a collection, you are already engaged in the analytic process as you inductively make judgments about what to include and therefore what to transcribe (see Chapter 3). For this reason, it helps to have a good grasp of the tools of conversation outlined in Chapters 4 and 5 before you do anything else. In addition, reading about your chosen area to explore findings from other CA researchers will allow you to identify gaps in the literature. Analysts might start by noticing something interesting or distinctive, which you can then use as a criterion for generating further instances. Instances can then be gathered into a collection, allowing for an increasingly refined description.

An initial collection will get you started, but then you may add or delete instances as you become clearer about your phenomenon. The process of building a collection can itself make what you are collecting become clearer. Analysis typically involves alternating between specific instances of a phenomenon or practice and consideration of its place in the wider collection. For this reason, the initial collection should be inclusive—it is better to include boundary cases and eliminate them (or not) through analysis. Later, the process of including or eliminating these cases provides a keener sense of your phenomenon. You should develop increasing clarity on what it takes to count as an instance of your practice—what features it has, what might look similar but actually be something else. You are aiming for sufficient precision that will allow you to clearly identify new cases as examples.

A useful discussion for data collection resources is the ethnomethodology and conversation analysis wiki list (http://emcawiki.net/Data_collection). Existing corpora of everyday talk are available at CA Bank (English, Spanish, Mandarin, others; https://ca.talkbank.org/) and the Language and Social Interaction Archive (English; http://www.sfsu.edu/~lsi/).

DATA MANAGEMENT

As you build your collection, it is important that you save the notes you make for each case. You might eventually use specialist software such as Transana or ELAN to do this (detailed later), but when starting off and for smaller collections, a basic computer folder structure can be quite sufficient. Figure 2.1 gives an example of a simple folder structure for a collection of threats in family mealtimes. When searching through the data corpus, each time we identified a candidate threat, we gave it a number and memorable name and cut out a video clip. We saved a transcript of the clip and another file of notes on the clip. Intensive analysis works with a collection of this kind.

As a study develops, it is often helpful to create a spreadsheet that codes features of instances. Table 2.1 gives an example of what this could look like in a repair project (see Chapter 4). The key is that the codes are produced

FIGURE 2.1. A Simple Folder Structure for Organizing a Corpus

Folders	Documents
01 whinging and wining	Crouch 08 if you want some pudding - notes
02 babies don't go to ballet	Crouch 08 if you want some p...ng you sit still in your chair.docx
03 quickly	
04 sit still	Movies
05 burping	fm08 if you want some pudding.mov
06 eaten enough	
07 there's no pudding	
08 use your spoon	
09 leave the table	
10 what mummy	
11 spits	
12 not talkin	
13 which one	
14 behavin badly	
15 baby forks	
16 carry on being good and not naughty	
17 stop it	
18 more of this	

by and make sense to the researchers and capture systematic features of the practice that is being explored. Each case is listed down the left column with a number and recognizable name (referring to the cases in Figure 2.1). The range of interactionally relevant features is listed across the top line, here different features of repair (see Chapter 5). This then allows you to order your cases and notice interesting patterns—for example, between different types of repair operation and position.

Software designed for data management in CA can take time to learn but can be useful if you have a large corpus of data to manage (discussed in Hepburn & Bolden, 2017). ELAN (https://tla.mpi.nl/tools/tla-tools/elan/) synchronizes recordings with annotations, and it can create multiple annotation tiers for representing talk, nonvocal conduct, and various linguistic features. However, ELAN does not fully support Jeffersonian transcription (outlined in Chapter 3). CLAN (https://dali.talkbank.org/clan/) can seem simpler but is less useful for manipulating video.

Transana (https://www.transana.com) is often recommended as an aid to transcribing and analyzing video and audio-recorded data. It supports the standard Jeffersonian transcription. Its major advantage is the ability to synchronize recordings with transcripts. It also has tools for coding data features and creating and exporting data collections. The screen displays the video, the transcript, and the waveform.

Although specialist software can be helpful for large collections, many CA researchers work primarily with Microsoft Word for transcription and Adobe Audition or QuickTime for managing audio or video files.

TABLE 2.1. A Table Showing a Simple Spreadsheet Structure

Case #	Trouble source	Solution	Initiation	Operation	Position	Framing
01 Interesting	Fun	Interesting	Cut off	Replacement	Mid-TCU	Preframed
02 Was he	Is he	Was he	Cut off	Replacement	Post-TCU	Postframed
03 Overdue	overdue	Long overdue	Cut off	Insertion	Mid-TCU	No
04 Restaurant	Restaurant	Restaurant	Stretch	Word search	Mid-TCU	No

Note. TCU = turn constructional unit.

SUMMARY

In this chapter, we have attempted to guide you through how to design and start to conduct your own CA. This initial process involves careful scrutiny of audio and/or video recordings, facilitating the generation of a collection across different episodes of naturally occurring interaction, a process that goes hand in hand with generating and refining research questions.

3 TRANSCRIBING FOR CONVERSATION ANALYSIS

There is a widespread assumption in social science research that simply writing out the words people say, as a competent copy typist might, can stand in for the interaction itself. Conversation analytic research recognizes the importance of not simply what people say but also how the delivery of what they say, combined with other bodily conduct, is fundamental to how actions are built and responded to. As conversationalists, we notice delays, changes of emphasis, tiny laughter particles, and words that are cut off and restarted, and we use these to ground our understanding of other people in real time—how they are feeling, whether they are being ironic, whether they are conveying something uncomfortable, and so on. For this reason, Harvey Sacks tasked Gail Jefferson, then a student of dance working as a research assistant for him, to transcribe his tapes. In close collaboration, she later built a full system that captures the rich subtlety of how we perform actions in talk and went on to produce a superb body of analytic work. Jefferson's system of conventions (Jefferson, 1978a; explained in detail in Hepburn & Bolden, 2017) was continuously informed by analytic developments that highlighted a growing set of features of talk that speakers themselves treat as relevant and that a simple verbatim transcript misses.

https://doi.org/10.1037/0000251-003
Essentials of Conversation Analysis, by A. Hepburn and J. Potter

In this chapter, we provide an overview of the key issues involved in getting started with your data and the key conventions used in transcribing. This will also allow you to read and hear how talk was produced for yourself. For further details, including illustrations of the importance of using the key conventions, and practical exercises, see Hepburn and Bolden (2017) and the accompanying exercises, which are open access (http://rucal.rutgers.edu/transcription/). You will get the most out of this chapter if you work on your own transcript of some materials and move between this chapter and these transcription exercises.

GETTING STARTED

Before embarking on transcription, it is important to consider (a) how much data you have and (b) the time you have available for transcription. For a novice transcriber, you can expect that for every 10 minutes of talk you have collected, you will have at least 2 hours of transcribing to do. Depending on the amount of time and data you have, it may be best to simply listen to your data first and generate a simple verbatim transcript. This has the advantage of tuning you in to your data and providing you with a searchable record of words and phrases. You may also add key descriptions, such as speakers' laughter or sounds of upset and anger—things that you think might be useful to follow up on.

TRANSCRIPTION CONVENTIONS

Jefferson transcription conventions are intended to build intuitively on familiar forms of literary notation (e.g., underlining for emphasis, capital letters for volume, arrows for pitch movement), which makes learning transcription conventions relatively straightforward. Like other chapters in this book, it is probably best to view this chapter as a manual rather than reading it as a continuous narrative. There is a lot of technical content! Following Hepburn and Bolden (2017), the conventions are organized under the following headings: transcript layout, speech delivery and intonation, and transcribing visible conduct.

Transcript Layout

Ignoring the rest of the aspects of speech delivery at this stage, Extract 3.1 illustrates five key features of transcript layout: (a) the extract heading typically has a number that allows easy reference (here, 3.1 is Chapter 3,

Extract 1), some kind of identifying title, and the time into the recording the extract starts; (b) lines are numbered; (c) each speaker transition is relevant (Sacks et al., 1974; see Chapter 4, this volume, for details), so a new speaker designation is given (e.g., Lines 01 and 02); (d) a fixed-width font is used (e.g., Courier) to align overlapping talk and/or visible behavior (at the end of Line 5 and the start of Line 6 then further into Line 6); and (e) a "gap" in talk (see the following section) is given its own line (Line 3).

Extract 3.1. The Schedule 07s

```
01 Syb:   ((to Glen)) Are we exercising,
02 Gle:   If you wa:nt,
03        (0.3)
04 Gle:   If you wanna take the week o:ff,=te like te work,
05 Hel:   Ye[ah:_]
06 Syb:     [Yeah] I think [(we'd) take t]he week off.
07 Hel:                    [(Think) Yeah.]
```

Temporal and Sequential Relationships

Conversation analytic researchers have shown the precision timing used by speakers. There is a range of temporal and sequential elements that we show the relevance of in Chapters 4 and 5 and that is detailed in Hepburn and Bolden (2017).

Overlapping Talk

Concurrent talk by two or more speakers is represented by lining the overlapping talk up and enclosing it with square brackets. The onset of overlap is shown by the left square bracket ([), the offset by the right square bracket (]), as in Lines 5 to 7 of Extract 3.1.

As we demonstrate in Chapter 4, precise transcription of overlaps and gaps shows that speakers routinely anticipate or, more technically, project possible completions of turn constructional units to start their talk at transition relevant places. Overlaps also expose a range of practices that speakers employ to subvert the normative rules of turn taking, such as one speaker at a time (see Chapter 4).

Latching

Latching is represented by equal signs (=) and shows the absence of a *beat of silence* (around 0.05–0.2 seconds of silence) routinely present in transitions between turns. It can occur between different speakers' turns:

Extract 3.2. Field:1:1:5

```
01 Les:   .hh Oh ↑by the wa:y Ann hasn::'u-sent Gordon anything,=
02 Mum:   =Yes she ha:s,
```

Within the same speaker's turn, a speaker "rushes through" to extend their turn after a possibly complete unit of talk (*turn constructional unit* [TCU]) has been produced:

Extract 3.3. Field:1:1:6

```
Mum:  Ah:.=But- .hh She sai:d (.) the reas'n why she hadn't had
```

Equal signs can also show that a speaker's talk, broken up into separate lines on the transcript to accommodate the placement of overlapping talk is, nevertheless, "through produced," as in Extract 3.4 (Lines 1–3):

Extract 3.4. Field 1:1:15

```
01 Les:  R[i:ght nh]=
02 Mum:   [↑Bye::: ]=
03 Les:  =↑↑Bye:,
```

Gaps and Pauses

It is important to distinguish between *gaps*, silences that occur between units of talk (by the same or different speakers), and *pauses*, silences within a unit of talk (Sacks et al., 1974). Gaps and pauses are measured to the nearest 10th of a second and shown in parentheses: between lines of talk for gaps (to show that speaker transition is relevant, whether or not it occurs) and on the same line as the preceding and subsequent talk for pauses. For example, Extract 3.3 has a *micropause* (.), which is less than 0.2 seconds. Extract 3.1 has a gap of 0.3 seconds on Line 03 (0.3), which will be in absolute terms up to half a second because it will include the beat of silence (around 0.1–0.2 seconds) that every normal transition between turns has (see Hepburn & Bolden, 2017, for more advice about timing silences). The gap shows that this is where a speaker transition could have occurred—in Extract 3.1, it does not occur; Glen resumes on Line 03.

SPEECH DELIVERY AND INTONATION

Important elements of speech delivery include unit-final intonation, stretches of words and phrases, cutoffs and jump starts, emphasis, volume, and pitch changes.

Unit-Final Intonation

Conversation analysis (CA) transcripts use punctuation marks (e.g., periods, commas, question marks, inverted question marks) to represent TCU-final intonation (not grammatical punctuation). Various researchers have shown that unit final intonation is part of action formation (e.g., Couper-Kuhlen & Selting, 1996; Golato & Fagyal, 2008; Schegloff, 1998). See Chapter 4 for more on action formation.

Specifically,

- a period indicates falling intonation;

- a question mark represents a strongly rising final intonation—not necessarily questioning, which can equally be done with a falling final contour;

- a comma indicates slightly rising intonation, which can, but does not necessarily, indicate that the speaker is continuing;

- an inverted question mark (¿) or a question mark followed by a comma (?,) indicates a final pitch rise that is stronger than a comma but weaker than a question mark; and

- an underscore (_) at a turn ending represents the same intonation through the TCU.

Volume

Underlining is used to indicate some form of stress or emphasis, either by increased volume or elevated pitch (often a bit of both). More underlining entails greater emphasis. For example, in Extract 3.5, Line 01, "study" carries less emphasis than when Helen says it on Line 02.

Extract 3.5. The Schedule

```
01 Gle:   For wha:t  (.)  t'study?=
02 Hel:   =>Study yah.<
```

Especially loud talk (e.g., shouting) is indicated by upper case. Degree signs are placed around stretches of talk that are quiet or soft or may precede single words. Double degree signs (°°) indicate a particularly quiet voice, such as sotto voce or whispering.

Pitch Variations

Variations in the pitch of talk are an omnirelevant feature of interaction (Couper-Kuhlen & Selting, 1996) and have been found to be relevant to sequential transitions (i.e., changing the trajectory of conversation; Stevanovic et al., 2017). It is useful to try to distinguish sharper rises or falls in pitch marked by the up and down arrows (↑ and ↓) from gentler pitch movements, which are not represented by arrows but can be marked by underlining, sometimes in combination with colon signs (which alone indicate sound stretching—see the following section). An underlined element followed by a colon indicates an up–down contour through the word. For example, in Extract 3.6, pitch moves from up to down through the production of the word "pa:ssing" (Line 01). An underlined colon indicates pitch movement sliding from down to up through the word (e.g., "les'n:s," Line 05):

Extract 3.6. Field:SO88:2:11:2.

```
01 Gle:  Yes I will[do. wh]en I'm: (.) when I'm next pa:ssing.
02 Les:         [ .hhh ]
03 Les:  .hhh Right. .h Now the other thing is, as part of his
04       Christmas presen:' I would like t'give Gordon a few
05       les'n:s=
```

Up and down arrows mark a more extreme change of pitch. Pitch variations can be marked within a word, as in "matt:↓ress:" in Extract 3.7, or across a string of words (surround the string with arrows), as in "↑we pl'se bring↑" in the following extract:

Extract 3.7. Wilson 02 15:25

```
01 Ellie:  Can ↑we pl'se bring↑ the matt:↓ress:.
```

Double arrows (↑↑ and ↓ ↓) can also be used for extreme pitch resets.

Speed or Tempo of Speech

The combination of greater than and less than symbols (> <) indicate talk that is compressed or rushed (Line 2 of 3.8, as follows).

Extract 3.8. MH 3girls Part1 16:10

```
01 BRI:  O:kay.=R'member <Va:l's fi:rst> (0.6) boyfriend¿=
02 LYD:  =.HHHHH! (.) >The cute one with the brown< hai:r¿
03 ASH:  The blonde [guy? ]
```

Used in the reverse order (< >), the signs indicate that the specified talk is more drawn out than the surrounding talk (Line 1 <Va:l's fi:rst>). This can add emphasis to talk.

The less than symbol (<) shows that subsequent talk is *jump started*, meaning it sounds rushed into, often with increased volume (and/or pitch) on the initial syllable as in Extract 3.9, Line 01:

Extract 3.9. TG, 18:36-43

```
01 Ava:  Well there's nothing else t'do.<↑I wz
02       thinkin[g  of  taking  the  car anyway.]  .hh
```

Here Ava quickly jump-starts into a new TCU line 01 ".<↑I wz".

Colons (:) show stretching of the sound just preceding them (see, for example, Extract 3.7 and 3.8, Line 01).

A hyphen (-) after a word or part of a word indicates an abrupt cut off sound:

Extract 3.10. Wilson 03 8:07

```
01 Mum:  ... I al:ways thought that people from Jamaica
02       were always bla- very dark skinned.
```

Here, Mum uses a cutoff in her self-repair (see Chapter 5)—she starts to produce "black" on Line 02 but then cuts herself off and replaces it with "very dark skinned."

Voice Quality

Space prohibits a full examination of other features of the delivery of talk relating to voice quality. The most common of these are

- smiley voice or suppressed laughter, enclosed or marked by "£";
- creaky voice (#); and
- tremulous voice (~).

Transcriber's Comments and Uncertain Hearings

Double parentheses are used to mark a transcriber's description of events: ((cough)), ((telephone rings)). Single parentheses are used to represent the transcriber's best guess (perhaps due to a bad recording or overlapping talk), as in Lines 06 and 07 of Extract 3.1:

Extract 3.1. The Schedule 07s

```
06 Syb:  [Yeah] I think [(we'd) take t]he week off.
07 Hel:                 [(Think) Yeah.]
```

FEATURES ACCOMPANYING TALK

The most commonly used features relate to aspiration, laughter, and upset.

Aspiration

Hearable aspiration (breathing) is shown by the letter *h*—more h's mean more extended aspiration. Hearable inhalation (in-breath) is shown with a period before the letter(s): ".hh". Hearable aspiration has been shown to convey a range of emotions—for example, extreme upset, panic, or hysteria:

Extract 3.11. Whalen & Zimmerman (1998, p. 148)

```
01 CT:  Nine=one=o[ne, what is your emergency?
02 C:            [HUHHHHH .HHHHHH HHHHHHH .HHHHH
03      HUHHHH .HHH ((loudly gasping/out of breath))
```

Laughing

Rather than being an indication of humor, Gail Jefferson (1984) showed that laughter can coordinate with and sometimes sustain difficult actions such as managing troubles telling. As Hepburn and Varney (2013) noted, laughter is typically made up of tokens such as huh, hah, heh, hih—that is, there can be different "voiced vowels" within aspiration, and as Line 03 in the following extract shows, the same speaker can use a variety of these.

Extract 3.12. Location, Location, Location

```
01 Phil:  [I don't    [think you're gonna give 'im]=
02 Hazel:             [a h H A H   H A ↑HA   ↑HAH ]=
03 Kir:   =[hih  ha  hah hah ha .h]  [i.h] h h]=
```

Laughter particles can contain (a) elevated volume and pitch (Line 02), with differing degrees of aspiration; (b) consonants (e.g., ".hugh" for a more guttural sound); and (c) interlacing with speech, with one or more elements of plosive aspiration (in parentheses; e.g., "thi(h)nk") or with "breathy" aspirations (e.g., "yeahh").

Crying

Features of crying can include (a) reduced volume, indicating trouble with speaking (as noted previously using degree signs); (b) sniffs (e.g., .shhih or .snih sounds); (c) other embodied features, such as touching the face and wiping the eyes, and hiding the face and avoiding eye contact; (d) silence, where other talk might be due (timed in seconds); (e) increased pitch (as noted previously using arrows); (f) increased aspiration (as noted previously, adding HHhh for aspiration); and (g) tremulous delivery, marked by surrounding the relevant talk with tildes (~). Hepburn (2004) showed that recipients are adept at noticing and responding even when only one or two signs of upset are present.

TRANSCRIBING VISIBLE CONDUCT

In face-to-face interactions, participants' visible conduct can be instrumental in how social actions are accomplished and coordinated, so where it is interactionally relevant, it must be represented on a transcript. CA researchers have relied on various methods (sometimes in combination) for transcribing visible conduct.

Visual Representations

Here, frame grabs (see Figure 3.1) can be edited, numbered, and embedded into the transcript at precisely the point that they occur, as in the following example, to show the speaker indicating the size of a dog to her friends:

Extract 3.13. Bodies

```
01 A:  like he's a chihuahua
02     but he's- this (0.8) like wi:de.
       ⇑1                    ⇑2
```

Transcriber's Comments

Transcriber's comments are placed in double parenthesis—such as ((A looks at B))—and aligned with the ongoing talk. In Extract 3.14, they are italicized

FIGURE 3.1. Numbered Frame Grabs Associated With Extract 3.13

Frame 1   Frame 2

to distinguish them further. They are probably the simplest way of transcribing visible conduct.

```
Extract 3.14. MH_3girls_Part1 16:10

01 ASH:   [↑OH [I↑ ↑↑KN]OW:!
02 LYD:        [WHA:T? ] ((jumping up, gaze to screen))
```

Specialized Systems

Here, each embodied action is surrounded from beginning to end by symbols and is precisely coordinated with other talk and symbols. Space constraints prohibit further elaboration, but Mondada's conventions are explained in a tutorial available online (see https://www.lorenzamondada. net/multimodal-transcription).

SUMMARY

Jeffersonian transcription is the standard system for representing talk-in-interaction in a way that crystallizes its interactional elements. In this chapter, the focus has been on vocal conduct in English language talk-in-interaction. Conversation analysts have increasingly worked on non-English materials, where transcripts facilitate shared understandings across multiple languages and cultures, allowing the identification of the structures of social action on a more global scale. Hepburn and Bolden (2017) discussed this further, along with the challenges of translation and transcription.

The benefit of a clear and accurate transcript is that it crystallizes interactional elements of talk in a way that provides easy access to the data, unlike audio or video records. As such, CA transcription is an essential resource for data sessions, presentations, and journal articles. It requires work to learn and takes time and focus to apply, but the result is a powerful platform for analysis.

4 TURN TAKING, SEQUENCE ORGANIZATION, AND ACTION FORMATION

As we noted in Chapter 1, our aim is to provide a practical analytic handbook that supports researchers as they work through a data set. In this chapter, we summarize three features of talk-in-interaction that are key tools in any analysis: turn taking, sequence organization, and action formation. We think of them as tools for analysis.

IDENTIFYING AND APPLYING THE TOOLS OF CONVERSATION ANALYSIS

In what follows, we present an overview of key elements of the basic machinery of talk. Once we understand those elements, we can use them as tools to unlock insights into what is happening in our data. The tools were developed from studies of how talk works. For example, turn-taking rules underpin the orderly production of conversation: how to stop speaking, how to select the next speaker, how to deal with someone else speaking at the same time (Sacks et al., 1974). We can use these to highlight how basic rules may be followed, restricted, or changed in institutional settings, such

https://doi.org/10.1037/0000251-004
Essentials of Conversation Analysis, by A. Hepburn and J. Potter

as news interviews (Heritage, 1998). Sequence organization shows how speakers get things done across a number of turns (e.g., Schegloff, 1968, 2007b), and action formation points us to the constituent practices that make up the basic task that a turn is performing (e.g., Levinson, 2013).

TAKING TURNS IN CONVERSATION

Have you ever been in a group of people and wondered who should speak next or why you are struggling to get in a word? These are the kinds of questions that the study of turn taking can help us answer. Sacks and colleagues (1974) set out some basic things about how most conversations work. Commonly,

- one person talks at a time rather than overlapping their talk with others,
- speaker change recurs, and
- there are typically small silences of less than 0.2 seconds between turns.

How do we manage to do these most basic but crucially important tasks? Since the 1960s, conversation analysts have developed extensive evidence that shows that listeners (often referred to as *recipients*) use features of the turn's unfolding construction to precisely *project* when and how to speak and that the speaking party may use a range of resources for allocating a turn to the next speaker. They have also shown the relevance of these findings across many different cultures (Stivers et al., 2009). Note that we often italicize key technical terms—let us unpack what we mean by speakers *projecting* when and how to speak.

The Projectability of Conversation

According to Sacks and colleagues (1974), there are three ways we can predict, or *project*, when it is our turn to speak next. We use

- grammar (e.g., where a complete sentence—"Do you like ketchup?"— has been produced),

- intonation (e.g., where the speaker sounds like they are adding more talk—"Do you like ketchup, or would you prefer some mayo?"), and

- action, where the speaker has produced a complete action (e.g., a question, compliment, complaint, invitation, or, as in the previous example, an offer of ketchup, such that their interlocutor can respond).

All these resources entail that we can project that an utterance is a complete *turn constructional unit* (TCU) and that it is our turn to speak next. Sometimes a single word will do in response ("Yes!"), sometimes a phrase ("What brand?"), and sometimes a full grammatical sentence ("I really love it!"). All these forms—words, phrases, sentences—would similarly count as a complete TCU—that is, each would form an appropriate responding action.

In another example, in Extract 4.1, Speaker B projects the completion of Speaker A's turn using action, grammar, and intonation and, following A's slight stretch on their final word, jumps in with a small amount of overlap to respond on Line 03:

Extract 4.1.

```
01 A:    Well if you knew my argument why did you
02       bother to a:[sk.
03 B:                [Because I'd like to defend my
04       argument.
```

The completion of a turn opens up what conversation analysts call a *transition relevant place* (TRP). At this point, the transition to the next speaker becomes relevant. So, here, we see Speaker B projecting an upcoming TRP.

Extract 4.2 gives another example. Here, the call taker (CT) hears the (0.8) pause on Line 04 as possibly showing the caller is in difficulty in completing her turn, so she projects a candidate ending for her on Line 05:

Extract 4.2.

```
01 Cal:  I'm afraidI d- I ↑fhind ↑myself very an:gry as
02       ~well as very~ ↑↑u.HHh ~↑very ↑ups:et.~
03       (0.2)
04 Cal:  Be↑cus (0.8) A[: h h ]
05 CT:                [It was] kept [from you:.]
```

Gene Lerner (1996) called this *anticipatory completion* and showed its relevance for different types of interactional projects (e.g., managing disagreement). So, in Extracts 4.1 and 4.2, we find evidence for the projectability of the first speaker's turn completion—in Extract 4.1, B projected the end of A's turn slightly early, and in Extract 4.2, the call taker projected where the caller's turn was headed and completed it for her.

In multiparty conversations, the rules of turn taking state that the first speaker can allocate who talks next by addressing them directly ("Jill, where's my sweater?") or indirectly ("How was the wedding?" if the speaker believes only one person in the group attended). If no one in particular has been selected, those present can self-select. If more than one person attended the wedding, then indirectly addressing them in this way might create overlapping talk (see the next section), where more than one speaker talks at once, or repair (see Chapter 5; e.g., "Who are you talking to?"). Finally, failing no next speaker talking next, the current speaker might continue. These findings might seem so obvious as to be not worth saying, but as conversation analysis (CA) researchers have shown (e.g., Waring, 2014), these aspects of *turn allocation* form the bedrock that can unlock information about what people do and how they do it in everyday life.

To recap: Turn taking describes a set of practices speakers can draw on to build and assign opportunities to speak. Actions themselves generally comprise TCUs, which are units of talk (sentences such as "Do you have any blue pajamas?", words such as "no," or phrases such as "only yellow ones"). A TCU needs to make sense to the recipient, both pragmatically and grammatically, and is usually marked by speakers as prosodically complete (see Chapter 3 for details). Recipients inspect the ongoing progress of a speaker's turn at talk and will typically project points of possible completion to progress a sequence smoothly. Being aware of how the turns are working and any deviations or restrictions is one key prerequisite for doing analysis.

Overlapping Talk and Interruption

As the rules of turn taking detailed by Sacks and colleagues (1974) showed, once a TCU has been produced by Speaker A, it is Speaker B's turn to talk, and a smooth transition can take place. However, as we saw in Extract 4.1, respondents can project the completion of a speaker's turn a little early, resulting in *terminal overlap* so that both speakers end up speaking at the same time. The following is another example:

Extract 4.3. (From SJS (1974), p. 702)

```
01 Desk:  What is your last name [Loraine.
02 Call:                         [Dinnis
```

In Line 2, the caller *misprojects* the ending of the Desk's turn, which could have been done after "What is your last name"—in other words, there was a TRP after the word *name*. Can we say that the caller designed this to interrupt the Desk's turn? No, this is clearly not a deliberate interruption because the caller comes in at a place where the prior turn could have been finished. Note then that a TRP may occur before the end of a speaker's unit of talk; this illustrates an important difference between a TRP and a TCU.

This is where CA gives us a way of distinguishing between, on the one hand, misprojections and terminal overlaps and, on the other hand, turns that are designed to invade the current speakers turn or, in vernacular terms, *deliberate interruption*. How does it do this? Compare Extract 4.3 with Extract 4.4, in which 14-year-old Virginia is arguing with her mom about how much her long-distance calls cost:

Extract 4.4. Virginia

```
01 Mom:   I think if you had to pay for your [jah-
02 Vir:                                       [You're
03        exa:ggera[tin' (it)]
04 Mom:            [pay for  ] your long distance
05        telephone calls you wouldn't make so many.
```

Here, Mom is clearly still in the middle of her turn on Line 01; indeed, she orients to Virginia's interruption by repeating parts of her turn on Line 04.

Multiunit Turns

So far, we have seen how people orient to one of the tacit "rules" of conversation—that speakers are entitled to one TCU, after which it is the other person's turn to speak. Of course, there are many departures, and it often happens that when we speak, we need more than one unit to make up a turn if, for example, we are telling a story or giving instructions. Does that disprove the whole turn-taking system? If we look closely at examples with multi-TCU turns, we see this kind of thing starting them off:

Extract 4.5.

```
01 Hyl:   D'you know w't I did t'day I wz so proud a'my[s e l]f,=
02 Nan:                                                [What.]
03 Hyl:   =.hh I we:nt- (0.2) A'right like I get off et work
04        et one,
```

As we will see in the following chapter, we typically do not just launch into telling stories without checking with other speakers; on Line 01, Hyla does a "story preface," essentially checking with Nancy whether she is on board with being told a story (see Extract 5.1 for how this pans out). In other words, we have various ways of securing more than one TCU—for example, by projecting a story or other kind of telling or being asked to explain or account for something. That does not change the fact that to get more than one TCU, something "extra" needs to happen—the norm is that speaker transition becomes relevant after one TCU, so extra work needs to be done to "buy" and/or grant an interlocutor more TCUs.

Departures from the rules of turn taking are one way we might infer psychological attributes about one another. For example, if someone cuts into your turn with heightened volume, you might infer that they are angry. If someone keeps taking more than one unit, you might consider them boring or selfish. The rules are normative; departures are regular and systematic but usually accountable in some way and, as such, are another resource for conversationalists to use.

TALKING IN SEQUENCES

So far, we have outlined the rules of turn taking used by speakers: We monitor one another's talk closely to determine when to take a turn and, indeed, who should take a turn. We use resources such as grammar, action, and prosody to do this (and gaze, where speakers are copresent; Stivers & Rossano, 2010). But this is not all we are doing—we also aim to figure out what type of action is relevant next—we are analyzing one another's talk. A greeting means that the next action should be a return greeting, an invitation means that some kind of acceptance or refusal is relevant, and so on. In other words, actions can be thought of in terms of sequences—pairs of turns or as a "course of action"—a request sequence, a complaint sequence, and so forth. The meaning of any action is dependent on both its content and the context in which it is uttered, and once uttered, that action creates a new context for what will follow. This provides a sequential structure that is normatively accountable; this means that if a speaker does not engage in an appropriate next turn—if, for example, someone has invited you somewhere or requested something, and you ignore them—it is an accountable issue. This is why we need to understand the sequential organization in which any action is embedded. This section illustrates the different types of sequences you might find in talk. We begin with the adjacency pair.

Adjacency Pairs

One principle at work in social interaction is that any particular turn at talk will be in some way eliciting and/or responding to a prior turn; any initiating action makes a responding action relevant. We call this pairing an *adjacency pair*—two turns by different speakers. We call them adjacency pairs because they are placed one after the other; so, an invitation makes acceptance or refusal relevant, a greeting makes a return greeting relevant. In CA, the first action is called a *first pair part* and the responding action a *second pair part*. We will just talk about first and second here. For example,

Extract 4.6.

```
01 Nelson:  Y'wanna drink?        (first: invitation)
02 Clara:   Yeah.                 (second: acceptance)
```

Extract 4.7.

```
01 MYR:  I'm dreadfully sorry,    (first: apology)
02 LES:  That's a'ri:ght,         (second: absolution)
```

The production of a first action makes a second action *conditionally relevant*— we say it is conditionally relevant because the second might not be produced, but if it is not, there is a "noticeable absence." Indeed, speakers strive to make sense of responses as responsive—for example,

Extract 4.8.

```
01 Nelson:  Y'wanna drink?
02 Clara:   It's raining outside.
```

Although Clara's turn does not look like it is responding to Nelson's invitation, Nelson will work to try and make sense of it in this context—for example, he might infer that Clara is using the rain as an excuse for refusing the invitation—this is due to "conditional relevance." We can think of this mutual display of understanding of what the other person "means" as a primary resource for exploring how intersubjectivity is sustained.

One form of evidence for this conditional relevance is to look for "deviant cases" that do not fit the pattern that initiating turns make responses relevant. One such deviant case reveals speakers pursuing responses when they are not forthcoming—for example, Lines 04 and 06:

Extract 4.9.

```
01 A:  Is there something bothering
02     you or not?
03         (1.0)
04 A:  Yes or no.
05         (1.5)
06 A:  Eh?
07 B:  No.
```

It can be a useful opening way into working analytically with an extract to break it up into basic adjacency pairs: Think which actions are starting something—firsts, and which are responding to something—seconds. When you do this, you will likely be faced with another fundamental feature of interaction: sequence expansion.

Sequence Expansion

It is often the case that actions do not simply arrive in neat two-part sequences. Instead, there can be a string of related turns that may initially seem hard to sort out. If this is the case, then it is likely that the talk contains sequences that have been expanded. In this section, we give a brief overview of what these are and what they are for. For a more detailed exploration of this, read Schegloff (2007b).

Table 4.1 shows how a basic adjacency pair can be expanded before, during, and after its production. We call these presequences, insert sequences, and postexpansion sequences.

Presequences

If we can hear that a first action is forecasting some other action—for example, checking availability or the newsworthiness of a story—then we can think of it as the first part of a *presequence*:

Extract 4.10.

```
01 Nelson:  Hi.
02 Clara:   Hi.
03 Nelson:  Whatcha doin'.
04 Clara:   Not much.
05 Nelson:  Y'wanna drink?
06 Clara:   Yeah.
```

The presequence here is Lines 03 and 04. "Whatcha doin'" is a first action that projects some kind of future action, such as an invitation or request. Clara's response on Line 04 gives what we call a *go-ahead* to that action. We can then call the actual invitation and acceptance on Lines 05 and 06 the *base sequence*—the action that was projected by the presequence. Schegloff (2007a) detailed other kinds of presequences such as pre-announcements (e.g., "Guess what") and prerequests (e.g., "Are you driving past the airport?").

TABLE 4.1. Sequence Expansions

Base sequence	Expansion
	Presequence
A. First part (e.g., invitation)	
	Insert sequence
B. Second part (e.g., acceptance)	
	Postexpansion

Why do we do presequences? One answer is that if Clara had blocked the presequence on Line 04 by saying, for example, "I'm just going out," then it is probable that Nelson would not have produced the base sequence, the invitation. Hence, presequences are useful in situations where one wants to avoid rejection by the other party.

Insert Sequences

Insert sequences are useful when the second speaker has some kind of problem with the first or needs further information before they can respond. For example, in Extract 4.11, B cannot respond to A due to a problem with hearing and so initiates "repair" (see Chapter 5) involving the insertion of a small sequence in Lines 02 and 03:

Extract 4.11.

```
01 A:  Have you ever tried a clinic?    Base First
02 B:  What?                            Insert First
03 A:  Have you ever tried a clinic?    Insert Second
04 B:  ((sigh)) No, I don't want to     Base Response
05     go to a clinic
```

These kinds of insert sequences indicate problems with what has just preceded—maybe caused by mishearing or failure to understand.

Postexpansion Sequences

Another way that basic adjacency pair sequences can be expanded is through a *postexpansion*. These can be minimal—third turns that finish the whole sequence, as in Line 04:

Extract 4.12.

```
01 Alice:  You wan' me bring you anything?
02         (0.4)
03 Betty:  No: no: nothing.
04 Alice:  Oh:kay.
```

Having secured a response to her offer, Alice closes the sequence with a version of "okay." Hence, for it to count as postexpansion, it is the first speaker who initiates the expansion. Here, its role is simply to close off this sequence and move onto a different topic.

Nonminimal postexpansions, by contrast, keep the sequence open a bit longer:

Extract 4.13.

```
01 A: How's your commercial.   Base First
02    (0.2)
```

```
03  R:  .hh It wuz fu::n.      Base Second
04  A:  Ye:ah?=                Postexpansion First
05  R:  =Ye::ah,               Postexpansion Second
06  A:  Easy money?            Postexpansion First
07  R:  Ee:zeee:: Mo:n:ey:.    Postexpansion Second
```

Here, the first speaker solicits information about R's commercial and pursues more information with two postexpansion sequences, the first on Lines 04 and 05, the second on Lines 06 and 07. One way to spot whether something is a postexpansion sequence or just a new sequence is to think about whether the initial speaker is treating the second, or response, as in some way insufficient. Here, A pursues a more detailed response from R, showing that "It wuz fu::n." is not sufficient. This also illustrates a broader point about analysis: In CA, we look to internal evidence in stretches of talk for claims that are being made. This evidence is often in the orientations that participants display as the talk unfolds—most basically, how they analyze one another's talk.

SUMMARY OF SEQUENCE ORGANIZATION

Sequence organization represents a set of practices that speakers use to order actions in talk into sequences. A sequence of talk has as its most basic element an adjacency pair, comprising an initiating action, or first pair part, and a responsive action, or second pair part. Such turns can be from a specific family or "type"—for example, a greeting "hello" makes a similar type of turn relevant: a return greeting rather than, say, sympathy or thanks. However, it is more often the case that turns are not symmetrically typed in this way, leaving speakers in a continual process of inspecting one another's actions—displaying their intersubjective understandings turn by turn at a speed that makes it look and feel instant and, where necessary, clarifying, correcting, or challenging one another. As we will see in the discussion of preference organization in the following chapter, this allows us an important window into how initiating and responsive actions can be designed to secure alignment. And this window is one that allows us to discipline our analytic claims about any interaction.

ACTION FORMATION

The primary tools that CA has discovered so far are the same tools that speakers use for building actions in talk—so far, we have covered turn taking and sequence organization, which are the most fundamental across different settings (Enfield et al., 2010; Schegloff, 2007b). We have shown that actions are built out of core practices such as TCUs, which are units of talk (sentences such as "Do you have any blue pajamas?" words such as "no," or phrases such as "only yellow ones"). We have also shown that, in analyzing one another's talk, we are projecting what type of action is relevant next—as 3-year-old Anna did when responding to Mum's "<u>Y</u>ou still got some ↑<u>bea</u>:ns left" in Chapter 1. In other words, actions can also be thought of in terms of sequences—pairs of turns or as a *course of action*—a request sequence, a complaint sequence, and so on. Schegloff (2007b, p. 7) referred to *action formation* in terms of these kinds of practices, producing an action that "can be shown to have been recognized by coparticipants as that action by virtue of the practices that produced it."

Participants in interaction need to know what action is underway so they can design their conduct and coordinate it with that action. The way actions are formed provides cues that enable that understanding. All the different elements of talk can be relevant here—timing, prosody, word choice, syntactical choice. And this understanding is continually and dynamically updated (it also provides a strong motivation for listening carefully to what people are saying). To illustrate,

Extract 4.14.

```
01 Amy:    It's your turn to walk the dog
02 Bill:   You've got your coat on.
03 Amy:    Yes, I got a bit chilly
```

We could analyze Line 01 as a kind of request and Line 02 as a refusal or counter request. However, it seems apparent in Line 03 that Amy understands Bill's turn not as a refusal and counter request but as soliciting an explanation for why she's wearing her coat. At this point in the sequence, it is not apparent to Amy whether she read this action right. We need the next turn in the sequence: Bill's response—for example, "No, I mean you should walk the dog." Hence, the basic tools of social interaction—the turns, sequences, and methods for checking and repairing misunderstanding—all contribute to the contextual variation and specification at the heart of social interaction. But how does "You've got your coat on" operate as the action of either requesting or soliciting an account? To answer this, we can introduce another element in our analytic toolkit: *epistemics*—how participants deal with issues of who knows what, in real time.

EPISTEMICS

Issues of who knows what are of continual practical concern in interaction and a central feature of action formation (Heritage, 2012). Are we giving people news or telling them what they already know? Can we show when we talk about a topic that the other party already knows about it? For obvious reasons, these questions are fundamental in interaction, so it is not surprising that there are developed procedures for managing them, which come under the general heading of *epistemics*. Here we focus on the knowledge claims that are built, defended, and contested in talk. There are often rights and obligations with respect to knowledge—the victim of a car accident has more right to talk about how much it shocked them, a model railway enthusiast may be expected to be able to talk knowledgeably about rail track layouts. Conversation has an elaborate apparatus that enables such relative rights and obligations to be indexed, and these features are different depending on whether you are in an initiating or responsive position in the sequence. Attention to asymmetries of epistemic access is particularly useful when analyzing institutional talk (Heritage, 2013).

One simple but important epistemic object in English is the particle "oh." A central use of "oh" is to validate the newsworthiness of something you are informed about (Heritage, 1984a).

Extract 4.15.

```
01 R:  I fergot t'tell y' the two best things that
02     happen' to me to'day.
03 C:  Oh super.=What were they
```

We can recognize Lines 01 and 02 as a classic presequence. It offers a telling—something that the speaker claims primary epistemic access to. And C's "oh" validates this as indeed new news (and the "super" picks up the positive nature of the news from the presequence).

These kinds of news receipts are common in everyday conversation but rarer in institutional settings such as courtrooms and news broadcasts. This is partly because of the institutional expectations of neutrality—"oh" validates the news as news, as unknown and partly because, in these settings, talk is produced for overhearers; it is not for the lawyer or news anchor to validate newsworthiness on their behalf. CA researchers sometimes talk of different settings having distinct *institutional fingerprints* where the presence or absence of news receipts, for example, or other normative practices can be an indicator of the distinctive nature of the setting (e.g., Hepburn et al., 2014).

Showing what you know and do not know is part of other conversational practices. For example, claims to partial knowledge can be used to "fish" for more information. The following is from the start of a phone call:

Extract 4.16.

```
01 Nan:  Hel-lo:,
02 Emm:  .hh HI::.
03       (.)
```

```
04 Nan:   Oh: 'i::: 'ow a:re you Emmah:
05 Emm:   FI:NE yer LINE'S BEEN BUSY.
06 Nan:   Yea:h (.) my u.-fuhh h-.hhhh my fa:ther's wife
07        ca:lled me,.hhh So when she ca:lls me::, .hh
08        I always talk fer a lo:ng ti:me cz she c'n
09        afford it'n I ca:n't.hhh[hhh ] °huh°]
10 Emm:                          [OH: ]::::::]:=
```

Here, Emma describes something that she has only partial access to: Nancy's line being busy means that Nancy is on the phone with someone. Nancy has primary epistemic access to this, Emma only secondary. Emma telling her (limited) side of things works to elicit Nancy's side. And indeed, "telling my side" is a generic technique for eliciting information in everyday settings (see Pomerantz, 1980). The strong newsworthiness of what is elicited is validated on Line 10 by Emma's loud and stretched news receipt.

CA researchers suggest that, in interaction, knowledge can be understood as having the character of a geographical terrain, with peaks and troughs (Heritage, 2012). In Extract 4.16, Emma has less knowledge about what Nancy was talking about on the phone; terminologically, this is referred to as Emma being *K*– (K minus); while Nancy has primary access, she is *K*+ relative to Emma.

Questions and answers are a central interactional form in which relative access to knowledge becomes live. Thus, if a speaker asks, "Who were you talking to?" they show themselves as K– relative to the recipient of the question, who is treated as K+. Using a tag question, "You were talking to John, weren't you?" in contrast, flattens the epistemic gradient because it presents a candidate understanding for confirmation by the recipient (who is still K+ but not as much relative to the questioner).

Things get more complex as we consider the design of questions. There is a major difference between *wh- interrogatives* (i.e., interrogatives starting with "who," "what," "when," "how," etc.) and *yes/no interrogatives* (e.g., "You were talking to John, weren't you?"), which invite the respondent to agree or disagree (yes or no) with some proposed state of affairs (Raymond, 2003). To reiterate, "Where are you going?" positions the speaker as K– on the epistemic gradient and positions the recipient as K+. When an answer is given, the questioner is moved from K– to K+.

Policing one another's epistemic access and the rights and obligations that go with it is an endemic feature of how utterances and the actions they transact will be understood. We have shown that one simple way that this can be illustrated is through question design. In many institutional settings, particularly where professionals work with clients of some kind, questions are a major part of the interaction. The growing body of work on question designs and the constraints they generate will be an important resource for analysts.

TIPS FOR APPLYING THE TOOLS IN THIS CHAPTER

Here, we summarize some key takeaway points that we use to help apply these tools:

Turn Taking

- Identify TCUs, and for each one, specify (a) what it is doing, (b) how it relates to prior TCUs, and (c) whether there are more than one in the turn.

- Identify turns, and for each one, specify (a) whether the speaker self-selected to get the turn or, if selected, by whom and (b) whether and how each turn relates to prior turns.

- Identify TRPs, and for each one, specify (a) whether the turn's talk extends past the possible start of the TRP and (b) whether and how the next speaker orients to the TRP.

- Identify any overlapping talk. Does it begin at a TRP? Is there evidence of disagreement? How is the overlap resolved?

Sequence Organization

Identify chunks of talk, and for each one, specify

- how each turn was initiated (first pair parts) and responded to (second pair parts);
- what the main action is;
- whether there are any expansions before (presequence), between the main action and its response (insert-sequence), or after the main action; and
- whether and how this chunk relates to other chunks of talk.

Action Formation

Identify where in the ongoing spate of talk your target action is:

- Ask yourself how you would respond in that context, and then focus on the way recipients respond—how are they treating it?

- Does the action seem tilted toward getting one type of response over another?

- Identify any points in the talk where knowledge is indexed or downplayed—for example, by focusing on different types of questions. For each instance, specify (a) the action being done; (b) whether the speaker is in first or second position; (c) where the speaker positions their access to knowledge relative to the recipient—for example, are they claiming K+, K−, or joint access?; and (d) what is achieved by indexing knowledge.

SUMMARY

Turn taking, sequence organization, and action formation are pervasive features of talk; they are key elements in how human interaction is managed. Because of this, they will inevitably play a significant role in any analysis that you conduct. In addition to the design of the turn and its position in the sequence, action formation can involve other elements of talk that we cover in the following chapter, as well as embodied resources of gaze and gesture and the overall context, institutional or otherwise, of the interaction. All these resources go into building actions such as requesting, complaining, disagreeing, noticing, and many more.

5 STORYTELLING, REPAIR, PREFERENCE ORGANIZATION, AND PERSON REFERENCE

In the previous chapter, we noted that the primary tools for doing any analysis of conversation were turn taking, sequence organization, and action formation. Whenever you analyze talk from a conversation analysis (CA) perspective, you will pay attention to speakers' deployment of these foundational tools. This chapter adds more tools for analysis that may or may not be present in your data: storytelling, repair, preference organization, and person reference. We cover each in turn.

NARRATIVES AND STORYTELLING

Most qualitative researchers are familiar with narrative analytic approaches that see narratives as individual objects tied to cognitive or cultural structures of one kind or another and, therefore, as objects that can be accessed by and downloaded into some kind of research instrument, most commonly an interview. From a CA perspective, we are focused on how narratives or stories appear interactionally in different settings, what occasions them, and what activities they accomplish. Hence, stories or narratives are seen as an

https://doi.org/10.1037/0000251-005
Essentials of Conversation Analysis, by A. Hepburn and J. Potter

organic part of the interactional environment and are typically studied under the heading of *storytelling*. People tell stories for a variety of reasons: to complain, boast, inform, justify, or just entertain. Story recipients are alert to the variety of different things that a story could be accomplishing. How stories are designed, constructed, and responded to depends in large part on what particular project is being implemented. And as we look at institutional settings, stories are generated for the purposes of psychiatric intake records, police suspect interviews, and clinical history taking and problem presentation.

If we focus on everyday settings, CA work has uncovered a number of shared elements—most important is that some of the rules of regular turn taking (most obviously, one unit of talk at a time) are suspended (Mandelbaum, 2013). Part of the task for a storyteller is bidding for this suspension. Note that long turns do not disprove the rules of turn taking— otherwise, why would we have to bid for their suspension?

In everyday talk, launching a story commonly involves a presequence or just a preface that bids for an extended, multi-unit turn (Sacks, 1972). This presequence often takes up some kind of stance toward what is to be recounted, thus preparing recipients for making certain kinds of responses (clearly, a story about a bad car crash will need different sorts of responses than a story about a surprise party). For example,

Extract 5.1. Hyla and Nancy

```
01 Hyla:   .Hhh D'you know w't I did t'day I wz so
02         proud a'my[s e l]f,=
03 Nancy:           [What.]
04 Hyla:   =.hh I we:nt- (0.2) A'right like I get
05         off et work et one,=
06 Nancy:  =Uh hu:h,=
07 Hyla:   =En I haf- (.) my class starts et two:. .hh
08         So within that one hou:r, I got tih school,
09         I parked I went .hh to the ba:nk, I hadda
10         stan'n the longest line deposit my che[:ck,
11 Nancy:                                         [Mm-hm,=
12 Hyla:   =.hhh I hadtuh go: into a:, (.) a camra store
13         t'get somethi:ng,=.hh en I, (.)we hadda wait
14         fer the shuttul bus, .hh got up tih school
15         en I bot my lunch, en I got tih clahhsss hh=
16 Nancy:  =Are you se:rious?=
17 Hyla:   =.hh No I made the whole thing up.'v course I'm
18         ser(h)i[ous.
19 Nancy:         [Wo::ow.=
```

Here, Hyla launches a story with a presequence on Lines 01 to 02. Nancy gives the "go-ahead" on Line 03, allowing Hyla an extended turn. One thing that the participants, like Nancy, have to figure out at this stage is what kinds of responses will be relevant here, and the stance incorporated in the presequence gives Nancy some clues—Hyla did something of which she was proud. Further clues appear in how the story presages achievements that can be completed in her lunch hour (Lines 07–14). Note three things here: First, the organization of a story is related to its local and specific recipients; it does not hang in the abstract—Hyla might tell the story differently, or not at all, to a different acquaintance. Second, during Hyla's telling, Nancy offers *continuers* "Uh hu:h" and "Mm-hm" at Lines 06 and 11. These display her hearing that the story is not yet done and show her attentiveness, in contrast with her "Are you se:rious?" (Line 16) and "Wo::ow" (Line 19), which offer "surprise tokens" (Wilkinson & Kitzinger, 2006), displaying her hearing of the story's completion and appropriately appreciating Hyla's achievement. Third, at the completion of the story, normal turn talking resumes, from Line 19 onward.

There are other different elements to storytelling—for example, how do story recipients know when a story is finished? One way to achieve this is to "return home," to use Jefferson's (1978b, p. 231) term. On Line 15, Hyla finishes with "I got tih clahhsss," which was projected as the boundary of the story in Line 07. Lerner (1992) also showed the detailed procedures for co-telling a story when three or more participants are present at each sequential position of a story's telling: story initiation, story delivery, and story reception. In this way, assisted storytelling elaborates on the basic sequential structure of dyadic storytelling. Finally, as Mandelbaum (2013) pointed out, more research needs to be done on the different practices used to tell stories in institutional settings and how these stories are designed for institutional purposes (see Drew & Heritage, 1992, for an elaboration on these issues).

REPAIR

So far, we have seen how speakers manage to coordinate their talk through the deployment of various turn and sequence organizational techniques and how that organization makes allowances for longer turns. But of course, this coordination does not always run smoothly: People say the wrong words, get confused, mishear, produce descriptions open to misinterpretation, and so on. In this section, we explore some of the techniques that people have for holding up the ongoing talk and "repairing" either themselves (*self-initiated repair*) or each other (*other-initiated repair*) in the pursuit of intersubjective alignment. *Repair* is a term first coined by Schegloff and colleagues (1977); they noted a range of practices that speakers have for holding up the progress of the talk to initiate and deal with possible trouble in hearing, speaking, or understanding.

We focus first on self-initiated repairs, where a speaker stops their ongoing progress to fix their own talk, and then other-initiated repairs, where a speaker displays some kind of trouble with the other speaker's talk (e.g., with hearing or understanding). The way these practices appear in different institutional settings and how they are formalized in one way or another is part of the distinctive institutional footprint that analysis will help identify. Mostly, we focus here on identifying and analyzing repair in everyday settings.

Steps in Identifying Repair in Interaction

We give examples, but the following are the questions that can be addressed in CA:

- How is the repair initiated? For example, does the repair appear in the same turn as the problem or trouble source or afterward? Is it the same speaker or a different speaker who initiates the repair? Different types of initiation can be cutoff sounds, pauses, uhms, and other disfluencies and/or stretches on sounds.

- What does the repair treat as the source of trouble or repairable? Here we can look for the repair solution, which might have "framing" that makes clear to the listener what is fixed (see Extract 5.2) or negations of the trouble source ("no" or "not x").

- How does it solve that trouble? Here, we can look for the repair solution and how it operates on the trouble source—does it replace it, reformulate it, insert a new word, and so on.

- What kinds of trouble are being dealt with by the whole repair segment? For self-repair, this might be some problem in producing a turn due to overlapping talk or saying something delicate or managing something difficult such as disagreement. For other-initiated repair, it might be a problem of hearing or understanding the prior speaker.

Table 5.1 illustrates the different types of repair organized in terms of where the repair is initiated relative to the trouble in speaking, hearing, or understanding—the "trouble source."

TABLE 5.1. Repair Organization

	Repair initiation	
Repair solution	**Self**	**Other**
Speaker of TS (self)	Self-initiated self-repair	Other-initiated self-repair
Recipient of TS (other)	Self-initiated other repair	Other-initiated other repair

Note. TS = trouble source.

Let's look at some examples of these to help identify the different elements that are important.

Self-Initiated Self-Repair

Extract 5.2.

```
01 Bee:  hh Hey do you see v- (0.3) fat ol' Vivian anymouh?
```

- In this fragment, we can see that Bee momentarily cuts off where she was heading—"v- (0.3)"—in other words, she holds up the progress of her turn to fix the trouble with what she is saying. This "v–" is the trouble source (maybe Vivian alone would not have achieved recognition).

- The v– cutoff sound is where the repair gets initiated by the speaker herself; hence, this is also the *repair initiation*. How is the repair achieved? What is the "solution" to the repair initiation?

- Bee adds "fat ol'" and then we have the reappearance of the v– sound in the production of "Vivian." This allows us to see that "fat ol'" is the *repair solution* and that it is "inserted" into Bee's ongoing turn.

- We say that this is a *self-initiated self-repair*, employing the *repair operation* of *insertion*—Bee initiates and fixes her own trouble; she "operates" on it by inserting more descriptive (and rather derogatory) detail.

The following is another example of self-initiated self-repair in a different position, using a different operation:

Extract 5.3. R4 Detainees

```
01 Int:  Didju not fee::l (0.2) sorry for the men.
02       (0.5)
03 Int:  For the detainee:s.
```

Here, the radio interviewer asks a challenging question: whether the prison guard (accused of torture) felt sorry for the Guantanamo Bay prisoners in their care. This question causes the guard some trouble, as we can see by the half-second gap following the interviewer's turn. As we saw earlier, speakers can project with remarkable precision when it is their turn to speak, and a gap of this kind usually displays some kind of trouble responding (Bolden et al., 2012). The interviewer deals with this failure by self-selecting to repair her prior description—instead of "men," she switches to calling them "detainee:s." Hence, she treats "men" as a trouble source and replaces "men" with "detainee:s," which becomes the repair solution. We know this because "detainee:s" gets preframed by the reappearance of "For the," allowing her recipient to hear this as being replaced rather than just adding more information. All of this happens after the possible completion of the interviewer's turn on Line 01 when it is the guard's turn to speak. Hence, this is a self-initiated self-repair, using the repair operation "replacement" in the transition space unlike in Extract 5.2, which occurred before the turn had finished.

Self-initiated self-repair is complex. Space does not permit us to list exhaustively the full range of self-initiated repair positions and operations, but see Schegloff (2013) for more detail.

Self-Initiated Other-Repair

Extract 5.4.

```
01 DAD:  O:::H yeah we went to thuh- (.) we went to uh: (.)
02 CIN:  Claim Jumper.
03 DAD:  Claim Jumper today.
```

Here, Dad initiates repair on Line 01; hence, it is "self-initiated," and he is in the midst of a word search when his daughter Cindy provides the repair solution "Claim Jumper" on Line 02. Hence, it is "other repair"—he comes up with the solution only after Cindy provides it. Note that this is one kind of *anticipatory completion* (Lerner, 1996) that we saw in Chapter 4—Cindy is not halting Dad's progressivity here; rather, she is providing a solution to his trouble in moving forward.

Other-Initiated Repair

In the example of an insert sequence in Chapter 4, we saw an other-initiated repair, reproduced as Extract 5.5. B cannot respond to A due to a problem with hearing, so B initiates "repair" with an insertion of a small sequence in Lines 02 and 03.

Extract 5.5.

```
01 A:  Have you ever tried a clinic?    Base first
02 B:  What?                            Insert first
03 A:  Have you ever tried a clinic?    Insert second
04 B:  ((sigh)) No, I don't want to     Base second
05     go to a clinic
```

Here, B gives an example of an *open class* repair initiation (Drew, 1997), meaning it treats the whole prior turn as problematic (meaning the solution is to simply repeat the trouble source turn, as A does on Line 03). This can be contrasted with more specific other-initiated repair types such as "tried a what?" or repeating the whole prior turn with questioning intonation, which does not display a problem of hearing and rather displays some other problem. Extract 5.5 provides an example of *other-initiated self-repair*; it is the speaker of the trouble source (A's Line 01) who provides the solution (A's Line 03). We can elaborate on the distinction between other-initiated self-repair and other-initiated other-repair by the following example:

Other-Initiated Other-Repair

Extract 5.6.

```
01 Ken:  An' they told me how I could stick a th-uh::
02       Thunderbird motor? (0.5) in my Jeep?=An'
03       I bought a fifty five [Thunderbird motor.
04 Rog:                        [Not motor, e:ngine.
05       You speak of [electric motor and a gasoline engine.
```

In this example, Roger both initiates repair on Line 04, targeting Ken's characterization of the "Thunderbird motor" (Line 02), and also provides the solution "e:ngine." This is *other-initiated other-repair*.

To summarize, repair happens when people manage trouble with either their own or their interlocutor's talk. An important first step in analyzing repair is identifying a trouble source. This then allows us to see how repair was initiated, what the solution was, and which operation (e.g., insertion, replacement) was used in producing a solution. It is crucial to hold in mind that repair is a participants' issue. As analysts, we are not judging participants against our standards; we are focused on what they identify, in particular contexts, as trouble. Repair has been used in a lot of environments to help explicate what is going on or to reveal new practices. It is precisely because repair highlights what participants orient to as trouble that repair can be a revealing analytic lever.

PREFERENCE ORGANIZATION

We have already considered turn taking and building action sequences. These give us a way to understand another basic conversational phenomenon: *preference organization*. Preference organization is a consequence of participants managing issues of *affiliation*, or agreement and disagreement. Consider simple adjacency pairs. Some initiating actions carry a preference for a certain type of response. For example, when you respond to an invitation or request, a preferred response is one where you cooperate with the course of action that the other person began. By contrast, rejecting an invitation or request does not cooperate with that course of action and often stalls it. The term *preference* is not meant to capture the psychological preferences of the participants. Whether you actually want to go to dinner or not, the preferred format of the response in conversation is acceptance—the key thing is that invitations are the kinds of actions that carry a preference of some kind. Table 5.2 illustrates the preference carried by other common actions.

Preferred Responses

We noted in our discussion of presequences that if we can hear that a first action is forecasting some other action (e.g., an invitation), then it requires some kind of "go-ahead" from the recipient of that action:

Extract 5.7.

```
01 Nelson:   Hi.
02 Clara:    Hi.
03 Nelson:   Whatcha doin'.
04 Clara:    Not much.
05 Nelson:   Y'wanna drink?
06 Clara:    Yeah.
```

When we considered this example in Chapter 4, we noted that "Whatcha doin'" (Line 03) is a preinvitation: a first that projects an invitation. Clara's second on Line 04 gives a go-ahead, making the actual

TABLE 5.2. Examples of Preferences Carried by First Actions

First action	"Preferred"	"Dispreferred"
Request	Agree	Decline
Invitation	Accept	Reject
Offer	Accept	Reject
Assessment	Agree	Disagree
Apology	Absolve	Assert or imply blame

invitation and acceptance on Lines 05 and 06 the *base sequence*—the action that the presequence prepared for. Presequences are useful for heading off rejections; rejections are *dispreferred seconds*. Extract 5.1 illustrates typical features of preferred responses. They are

- immediate—beginning right after the transition relevant place (sometimes slightly earlier),
- unqualified—lacking in hedging or mitigation (compared with Extract 5.8), and
- nonaccountable—speakers do not need to explain why they are accepting.

Dispreferred Responses

The typical form of an acceptance (preferred) can be contrasted with what happens with a rejection or disagreement (dispreferred).

Extract 5.8.

```
01 R:  And uh the: if you'd care tuh come ovuh,
02     en vis↑it u little while this morn↑ing
03     I'll give you[cup a' ↑coffee.
04 B:             [ khhh
05 B:  Uhhh-huh hh W'l thet's awf'lly sweet of yuh
06     I ↑don't think I c'n make it this morning,
07     hheeuhh uh:m (0.3) tch I'm running en a:d in the
08     paper 'nd an:d uh hh I haftih stay near
09     the pho::ne,
```

In this extract, B's rejection (Line 06) has a number of typical elements common to dispreferred next actions. First, it is delayed by some outbreaths and appreciation for the invitation: "thet's awf'lly sweet of yuh." It is also qualified: "I ↑don't think" (Line 06), making it seem slightly less definitive. In addition, "this morning" (Line 06) further qualifies the rejection. It makes the rejection conditional on the timing and implies that, at another time, it would be accepted. It also includes an account for the rejection "running en a:d in the paper . . . haftih stay near the pho::ne."

To summarize, *dispreferred responses* are typically

- delayed—they have gaps before responding, hesitation markers (e.g., "Well" or "Uh::"), and expressions of appreciation;
- qualified—the response softens the negative quality of the dispreferred by being indefinite, uncertain, conditional; and
- accountable—the response is explained, excused, and justified.

The regularity of these features of dispreferred responses means that recipients can predict what is to come. This can allow them to engage in various preemptive actions, such as offering inducement:

Extract 5.9.

```
01 A:  Oh I was gonna sa:y if you wanted to:, ˙hh
02     you could meet me at UCB and I could show
03     you some of the other things on the
04     compu:ter,
05     (.)
06 A:  Maybe even teach you how to program ba:sic
07     or something. .hhh
08     (0.6)
09 B:  Well I don't know if I'd wanna get all that
10     invo:lved,
```

Here, following the micropause on Line 05, A upgrades their initial offer to provide technical help. Speakers routinely hear delays following offers or requests as prefiguring turndowns. This advanced warning gives them the opportunity to build in further inducement, in this case, adding extra help to the offer. Another typical pattern would be to add something after the gap on Line 05 that "reverses the preference," such as "Or don't you have time?" This practice is done to make it easier for the interlocutor to refuse the offer (Pomerantz & Heritage, 2013).

It is important to note that these design features are not "psychological" preferences, nor are they idiosyncratic to specific speakers. For example, they have been observed across a range of sequences involving disagreement and disconfirmation (Pomerantz, 1984; Sacks, 1987) and also corrections (Schegloff et al., 1977), as well as personal assessments (Pillet-Shore, 2012). It is also important to note that disaffiliation without elements of preference organization does not disprove the existence of these mitigating practices; rather, it provides a key to unlock something interesting, such as a close relationship, teasing, or more severe breakdowns in affiliation.

Summary of Preference Organization

Preference organization describes a set of practices for maintaining agreement and social solidarity, as well as managing disagreement. In identifying preference organization, it is important to ask yourself whether there is a first action that presents the recipient with a choice between cooperating or not cooperating with a course of action. With noncooperation, can we identify elements of a dispreferred response, such as some kind of delay, qualification, mitigation, or providing accounts? You can also look for attempts by the speaker of the first action to deal with potential trouble ahead, perhaps by offering inducement or reversing the preference. Pomerantz and Heritage (2013) elaborated on these and other forms of preference organization—for example, dispreferred initiating actions. In the following section, we see that there are also broader preferences that have been identified in relation to how people refer to one another.

PERSON REFERENCE

There are many different ways of referring to people (e.g., my brother, a man, a gardener). Why select one form rather than another? This is an area of interaction where systematic and revealing practices have been studied—for example, in the choice between a name and a description (Schegloff, 1996). Here, we only have space to offer a glimpse into the work that is done by the use of different reference forms. We start with reference to others.

There are two principal ways of making such a reference: either by using a recognitional form or a nonrecognitional form. When a speaker employs a *recognitional reference* in interaction, they convey to their recipient an expectation that the person they referred to is known to them. This can be done simply by using a name (e.g., "I saw Helen Smith yesterday"), or it can be done through a recognitional description (e.g., "I saw the woman who taught us History"). *Nonrecognitional reference* might be done through "I saw this woman" or "I saw my History teacher."

Preferred Reference Forms

We can understand the use of preferred reference forms in terms of preference organization. There are two preferences at work when referring to others (Sacks & Schegloff, 1979). First, there is a preference for using a recognitional over a nonrecognitional reference form; second, there is a preference for minimized reference forms. Both of these preferences are usually achieved by selecting a name, where one is available:

Extract 5.10.

```
01 A:  It's John.
02     (0.5)
03 A:  Smith
04 B:  Ah Hi John!
```

Here, the addition of the last name is done as an *increment*—an addition to the prior turn—indicating that A expected the recipient to secure identification with just a first name. The preference for minimized reference operates here in the initial minimal selection of just a first name. The *preference for recognition* operates such that if the speaker knows that the recipient knows the person referred to, they should select a recognitional reference (e.g., the person's name) rather than a nonrecognitional description (e.g., "this friend of mine"; Schegloff, 1996).

Sacks and Schegloff (1979) showed how, when these two preferences come into conflict, achieving recognition takes priority over the preference for minimization. For example, in the following segment, the speaker adds multiple referring expressions, finally relaxing the preference for a minimal reference in favor of achieving recognition:

Extract 5.11. NBII:1:R:6

```
01 Emm:   But PERcy goes with (.) Nixon I'd sure like tha:t.
02 Lot:   Who:?
03 Emm:   Percy.
04        (0.2)
05 Emm:   That young fella thet uh (.) .hh his daughter wz
06        m:urdered?
07        (0.5)
08 Lot:   .hhh [OH::: YE::AH:. YE:A[H. y-]
09 Emm:        [They-            [They:] said sup'n abou:t...
```

Here, Emma's initial referent "Percy" does not secure recognition by Lottie, even after repetition on Line 03. This leads to further expansion into a *recognitional descriptor* "That young fella thet uh (.) .hh his daughter wz m:urdered" on Lines 05 to 06, which, as Sacks and Schegloff (1979) predicted, is *try marked*—offered as a try—with questioning intonation. This neatly displays the two preferences in action: first, a minimal name reference, then a repetition, both of which illustrate the preference for minimization. Only after these have not worked, a recognitional description is used on Lines 05 to 06. If it worked the other way— if the preference for a minimized reference took priority—then a minimal nonrecognitional reference (e.g., "some guy") would be selected.

In contrast, nonrecognitional reference forms do little else but convey nonrecognizability (e.g., "I saw someone/this man/this woman"—not someone you know). More elaborate nonrecognitionals include further description (e.g., "I saw a guy from work"). The distinction between recognitional and nonrecognitional needs to be supplemented by a further distinction, between locally initial and locally subsequent reference forms.

Locally Initial and Locally Subsequent Reference Forms

To illustrate this distinction, take this example from a child protection helpline—the caller is phoning a child protection officer (CPO) to report suspected abuse. We are right at the start of the call:

Extract 5.12. DG Abusive Mum

```
01 CPO:     Okay, go ahea:d,
02 Caller:  Right I've- (.) e-I've got (.) e-a concern about
03          a lady. She keeps sayin to numerous people:, .hh
04          that she's been interferin wiv 'er kids:.
05          (0.7)
06 CPO:     She's actually: talking about this.
```

Here, we have three different nonrecognitional reference forms in bold. All are locally initial reference forms in locally initial position—that is, they are the first references to people. We also have three (italicized) locally subsequent reference forms "she," all referring to the "lady" who is the topic of the call. They are all in *locally subsequent* position, meaning they occur, as is normal, after the production of the *locally initial* reference form. Deviations from this standard pattern can be revealing interactionally (e.g., Kitzinger et al., 2012) or may simply be subject to repair, as in Line 02:

Extract 5.13. [Rahman:B:2:JV(14)]

```
01 Vera:  I thought you could'a called up for coffee.
02 Jen:   Oh::::. Have they have your visitors g[one then,]
```

Because Vera's visitors have not been mentioned up to this point, Jenny repairs her use of the locally subsequent "they" to a locally initial recognitional description "your visitors."

A further important distinction is between marked and unmarked forms of person reference. Here, the distinction turns on what actions speakers are performing with a particular reference form. For example, in "Where's Helen?" the reference form does no more than provide for the recognition that allows the question to be understood. "Helen" in locally initial position is an *unmarked* formulation. Similarly, self-reference is produced in unmarked form in Line 02 of Extract 5.12: "e-I've got (.) e-a concern"—referring to oneself as "I" is just the normal simple way to do it in both initial and subsequent position (Schegloff, 2007c). A reference is unmarked if nothing special is being done with that reference.

By contrast, referring to a person who is known to both speaker and recipient by name using an alternative means of recognitional reference (e.g., "Where's her majesty?") may convey that something more than referring, possibly negative or teasing, is being done. Hence, these *alternative recognitional reference forms* (e.g., her majesty) are *marked* formulations.

Other ways of doing marked formulations include using a locally initial reference form in locally subsequent position:

Extract 5.14.

A: You didn't come to talk to **Karen**?
B: No **Karen** and I are having a fight.

Here, B could have said, "She and I are having a fight" but instead selects the nonnormative locally initial form. This is one way that speakers mark that something extra is being done other than simply referring to it (e.g., starting a new topic). Alternatively, a locally subsequent form can be used in a locally initial position to make a point—for example, walking into someone's house and asking, "Is he home?" where no prior reference to that person was given.

Marked reference forms can also appear when referring to oneself— for example, when a speaker refers to themselves not as "I" (the unmarked form of self-reference) but as "the woman he fell in love with" (Hepburn et al., 2012)—and provide a flexible resource for accomplishing a range of social actions.

Categories and Attributes

One way of referring to others is to select a category in which they are a member. Each of us has many available categories that can describe us— young man, teacher, Buddhist, gay man, Democrat, cat person, and so on. One of the revealing things in interaction is which membership category is selected and when and what is achieved by that selection. Categories often hang together—mommy, baby, sister, and so on—and imply certain sorts of skills, knowledge entitlements, or behaviors. Category selection may also be treated as indicative of the speaker's assumptions or social position, providing ways into exploring what most social theorists think of as psychologically (rather than interactionally) located biases and stereotypes.

Just as reference to others is not necessarily done using membership categories, equally, membership categories are often deployed in the service of doing something other than referring to a person. Schegloff (2007c) showed that the important questions about categories we need to ask ourselves when doing analysis are what is doing the referring, what is doing the describing, and what is doing the categorizing. He gives the following examples to illustrate these differences:

Extract 5.15.

```
01 Bee:   nYeeah, .hh This feller I have-(nn)/(iv-)
02        "felluh"; this ma:n. (0.2) t! 'hhh He ha::(s)-
03        uff-eh-who-who I have fer Linguistics=
04        =[is real]ly too much, .hh[h= ]
05 Ava:    [ Mmhm? ]                 [hm,]
06 Bee:   =I didn' notice it b't there's a woman in my
07        class who's a nurse 'n. .hh she said to me
08        she s'd didju notice he has a ha:ndicap en
09        I said wha:t. You know I said I don't see
10        anything wrong wi[th im, she says his ha:nds.=
11 Ava:                     [Mm:.
```

Bee's turn across Lines 01 to 07 contains category terms used in nonrecognitional reference forms: "feller," "ma:n," "woman," "nurse." However, the "feller or man" who Bee has for Linguistics "has a ha:ndicap." Although "handicapped" could be a category term, here it is a description of Bee's linguistics teacher's attributes. Compare this with the following example, however, where we see the term being deployed as a category term in Line 2:

Extract 5.16.

```
01 Bee:   [Yihknow] she really eh-so she said you know, theh-
02        ih- she's had experience. .hh with handicap' people
03        she said but .hh ih-yihknow ih-theh- in the fie:ld.
04        (0.2)
05 Ava:   (Mm:.)
06 Bee:   thet they're i:n[::.=
07 Ava:                    [(Uh [huh)
08 Bee:                        [=Yihknow theyd- they do
09        b- (0.2) t! .hhhh they try even harduh then
10        uhr-yihknow a regular instructor.
```

Here, "handicap' people" are referred to collectively, such that taken-for-granted knowledge gets deployed about members of the category—people like that try even harder. A key issue here is, therefore, whether someone specific is being referred to by the use of a category or, as in this example, whether the category is being used to describe a collectivity.

The following example illustrates a further important distinction, that between recognitional references and category terms. Here "**DeWald**" (at Line 03) and "**Keegan**" (at Line 07) are recognitional references referring to persons known in common. Schegloff (2007c) contrasted this with "a'pits'r fulla *Keegans*" at Line 07 or "a *Keegan*" at Line 08 or "a' *Fra[:nks*" at Lines 09 and 10. Here, we see family names that were previously referring to specific persons known in common suddenly being used as category terms to refer to a collection of people that have that category in common.

Extract 5.17.

```
01 Mike:  So:mebuddy rapped uh:.
02 Curt:  ((clears throat))
03 Mike:  DeWald'nna mouth.
04 Curt:  Well, h[e deserved it. ]
05 Mike:        [But yihknow eh-] uh-he made
06        iz first mistake number one by messin with
07        Keegan because a'pits'r fulla Keegans en
08        when there isn't a Keegan there ere's
09        a'Fra[:nks, ]
10 Curt:       [ Mmhm, ]<There's a Fra:nks,
```

There is an entire subfield related to CA that studies the systematic properties of category usage (Schegloff, 2007b, 2007c) and offers incisive commentaries on what is involved in doing this kind of analysis. Some good examples include Whitehead and Lerner (2009), who explored the deployment of different categories of racial membership, showing how the mundane invisibility of Whiteness routinely and recurrently reproduces asymmetrical relationships between category use. Kitzinger and Rickford (2007) also showed how referring to people as members of gendered categories constitutes, rather than reflects, a preexisting gendered world.

Summary of Person Reference

There is a fundamental question when you are analyzing references to or about people, and this also applies to places, times, events, and so on. The question is, as a speaker, how does one convey either that nothing more than referring is being done or that something else in addition to referring is being done? If we are thinking specifically of referring to persons, there are distinct sets of practices. We know that references to persons are often not done by membership categories, and membership categorizations are often deployed in the service of actions other than referring. It is important to ask what is doing the referring, what is doing the describing, and what is doing the categorizing.

INTEGRATING AND APPLYING THE ANALYTIC TOOLS

Having established an understanding of some of the basic tools of talk-in-interaction in this and the previous chapter, our goal is to apply them analytically. But where do we start?

In Chapter 2, we discussed how developing research questions goes hand in hand with understanding what we are looking for. We noted that most CA collections are of either a practice, a social action, a specialized activity, or some hitherto unnoticed technical feature of social interaction. For example, for institutional data, this might be specialized activities such as advising or empathizing or history taking; for more basic CA, this might be discovering new technical analytic features (e.g., new forms of repair), for practices this might be uses of turn initial address turns or prefacing turns with an "oh."

Heritage (2010) offered a useful discussion of the steps that go with the development and refinement of his analysis using his work on "oh" in interaction as an example. He takes the reader through the process of refining oh-prefacing down to a study that focuses on oh-prefaced responses to questions, and he shows how the analysis supports the claim that oh-prefaced responses convey something inappropriate or unexpected about the initiating question. He walks the reader through various decision points: first, whether a practice is distinctive; second, locating it sequentially; and third, determining the evidence—do speakers orient to it as having that distinctive role? The following is one of his examples that illustrates this last issue—having located a distinctive practice (oh-prefaced responses to questions), how do we find the evidence that participants orient to it?

Extract 5.18. Frankel QC:I:2SO:1

```
01 Ann:  How are you feeling Joyce.=
02 Joy:  Oh fi:ne.
03 Ann:  'Cause- I think Doreen mentioned that you weren't so well?
04       A few [weeks ago:?]
05 Joy:        [   Yeah,  ] Couple of weeks ago.
06 Ann:  Yeah. And you're alright no:[w?
07 Joy:                              [Yeah.
```

Here, we have an oh-prefaced response to an inquiry on Line 02. If oh-prefaced responses to questions imply that the answer to the question is obvious or self-evident, we might expect some kind of orientation to this by the questioner in the postexpansion sequential position. Heritage points us to Lines 03 to 04, where Ann defends her initial question by reference to what "Doreen" told her about Joyce's ill health. Joyce confirms that she had been unwell a "couple of weeks ago" (Line 05). Attending to the turn design, the sequential position, and the display of epistemic access give us important insights into a practice—something that has a specific function that we can apply across different contexts.

We can illustrate the application of our CA tools further by walking through a piece of analysis. Let's say you are interested in news announcements—this could be in clinical settings where we might want to focus on delicate and challenging actions such as breaking bad news, or it could be in everyday conversation, as the following, in which two friends are talking on the phone. Ann has just come back on the line after taking another call:

Extract 5.19.

```
01 Ann:    Maya?
02 Maya:   Ye:[s.
03 Ann:       [You wouldn't believe who that was.
04            (.)
05 May:    Who:.=
06 Ann:    =↑Rachel.
07 May:    Oh my ↑go:d.
08 Ann:    I ↑kno:w.
```

If we are thinking of locating news announcements sequentially, the first thing you might notice here is the presequence initiated on Line 03. This illustrates how coparticipants work to establish news as news through the sequential design of talk. By definition, a piece of news should be something "new" to the recipient, and so preannouncements are a useful check in this context. As we saw in Chapter 4, presequences can be a resource for speakers to establish recipiency for their main action. The "go-ahead" on Line 05 from Maya indicates that she does not already know the news and is ready to hear about it. Another feature of the presequence important for this example is that it indicates to the recipient precisely how they should hear this news. Is it good news or bad news? (See Maynard, 1997, for more examples.) Here, "You wouldn't believe" in Line 03 lets Maya know that some display of surprise might be an appropriate next turn. Maya's response on Line 07 is hearable as conveying that (Wilkinson & Kitzinger, 2006) and is acknowledged by Ann as a shared response to her news with "I ↑kno:w" on Line 08, conveying that they are on the same page (Mikesell et al., 2017). Note that we have cited three studies here, all of which have found distinctive practices related to news announcements and the responses they can make relevant.

In the course of our analysis, we can also deploy our understanding of person reference: We can notice that the use of a first name, "Rachel," is designed to indicate someone known to both speaker and recipient. Does Maya know Rachel? Maya's animated response, "Oh my ↑go:d!" (Line 07) with its elevated pitch and stretch on "god" suggests she does. This would be an opportunity for repair (via an insert sequence) if there were a problem (e.g., "Rachel who?"), but no repair is initiated. As Local (1996) suggested, turns such as "oh, god," "oh, no," and "oh, wow" are *assessment formulations* that in some way deal with or evaluate whatever the prior informing has been. And as we saw in the discussion of epistemics in Chapter 4, Heritage (1984b) discussed the function of "oh" as a *change-of-state token*—it works interactionally to show the speaker has undergone a change from not knowing to knowing (from K– to K+, as we noted in Chapter 4). So "surprise" and "assessment" are actions that Maya can be seen to be performing. She responds appropriately—appreciating the surprising news. The whole sequence reveals an orderly and compact way of transacting some interactional business.

The analysis of this one short extract also illustrates the relevance of a number of the tools that we have outlined in this and the previous chapter. From the general start point in asking how people deliver news to one another, we can start to see different ways forward and also the different ways that other conversation analysts have approached this topic. For example, we could collect a set of "surprise tokens" following news announcements. This might tell us interesting things about "surprise" as an emotion (Wilkinson & Kitzinger, 2006) or about responding to news more generally. It may also tell us how presequences can be used to characterize news in ways that forecast what type the news is—surprising, worrying, and so on (Maynard, 1997)—or how insert sequences target minimal person reference forms.

Here, we summarize some takeaway points that will help you apply the tools in this chapter.

Repair

- Identify any self-initiated same-turn repairs, and for each one, specify (a) repair initiation, trouble source, repair solution; (b) the repair operation(s); (c) what the repair achieves interactionally; and (d) whether there are more than one in the turn.

- Identify any other-initiated repairs, and for each one, specify (a) what type it is and (b) what, if anything, it does beyond just indicating a problem with hearing or understanding.

Preference Organization

- Identify any initiating turns (first pair parts) that appear to carry a preference for one kind of response over another.

- Specify whether they get preferred or dispreferred responses, and note whether there are any elements of dispreference in their responses specified.

- Identify any preferences related to person reference—for example, preferences for using a recognitional over a nonrecognitional reference form or preferences for minimized reference forms.

Person Reference

- Identify any references to persons and specify whether they are locally initial or locally subsequent, recognitional, or nonrecognitional.

- Identify any positional misalignments (e.g., locally subsequent in locally initial position or vice versa) or nonrecognitional terms where both parties clearly understand who is being referred to. What can be said about the selected usages?

- Identify any marked reference forms and think about why these forms were selected.

- Identify any membership category terms and specify whether they are doing describing, categorizing, or referring to a particular person or collective.

- Can you show what is achieved by the choice of this category term versus some other?

Synthesizing the Analysis Before Writing Up

- Prepare an outline of the data in a way that illustrates your phenomenon.

- For each extract, include

  - a transcript as set out in Chapter 3,

  - some context: Why this extract? Who are the speakers? What just happened?

  - a line-by-line analysis of the emerging phenomenon and its sequential position,

  - how this extract advances your general case for this section of your outline, and

  - your extracts organized into sections in a way that develops your ideas.

SUMMARY

We have shown the many ways that speakers deal with problems of speaking, hearing, or understanding the ongoing interaction and the implications of different ways of referring to or categorizing ourselves and others. We have also explored how interlocutors can organize sequences to maintain affiliation through preference organization and to facilitate longer turns such as storytelling. The reason that these are useful tools is that, as many studies in CA have shown (e.g., see chapters in Sidnell & Stivers, 2013), their logic appears to operate across all interactional contexts—from dinner tables to therapy sessions, from emergency helplines to classroom interaction.

6 WRITING THE MANUSCRIPT

Although the surface organization of conversation analytic papers varies, the underlying logic is standard. The aim is to document the existence and uses of specific social actions (e.g., apologizing, complimenting) or a conversational practice or other specialized activities, such as delivering a diagnosis. A basic methodological principle of conversation analysis (CA) is that, as far as possible, the reader should be put in the position of the analyst, so they can fully evaluate the claims made. The reader needs to see how conclusions link to specific features of the materials being studied. In this chapter, we describe the main features of a typical CA paper.

INTRODUCTION

As in all quality research, good CA papers have a pithy and clear title and an accessible abstract to summarize the research. The problem or topic of the paper is introduced in the context of a review of existing CA literature. The boundaries of that literature are not always clear-cut, but the majority of CA publications will be captured in the ethnomethodology and CA bibliography

https://doi.org/10.1037/0000251-006
Essentials of Conversation Analysis, by A. Hepburn and J. Potter
Copyright © 2021 by the American Psychological Association. All rights reserved.

on the wiki page. The introduction will typically give a broad introductory gloss on the analytic topic. This may cover prior non-CA literature. Where the study is addressing a topic that has been dealt with by mainstream psychological or clinical research, some brief coverage of that research may be required. For example, a CA study of assessments might start with a consideration of how attitudes have been conceptualized in social psychology (Potter et al., 2020); a study of threats might review work on social influence (Hepburn & Potter, 2011). It will introduce the practice that is to be studied in the paper and what is interesting about it.

METHOD AND MATERIALS SECTION

CA is an approach centered on a particular way of doing analysis. For that reason, papers in journals that welcome CA studies typically do not devote space to method beyond stating they are doing CA. For journals where the readership may be unfamiliar with CA, it may be important to outline what it is and the particular elements of CA that you are drawing on. For example, a study exploring speech and language therapy might be particularly focused on repair practices, so explaining these for the CA novice will be important.

If the researchers are doing basic CA, they will probably draw on one or more of a series of commonly used data sets (see Chapter 2 web links to some data resources). These have the virtue of having had hundreds of hours of high-quality transcription already been done on them. Often, researchers or research groups will collect more of their own materials to add to the available pool. The aim is to document generic practices that are widely shared rather than pursue a more sociolinguistic project of identifying differences between classes, regions, or genders. Once a practice has been clearly identified using CA, this would then be a much stronger, more nuanced platform for considering how the practice is distributed across different social groups (as seen in Speer & Stokoe, 2012).

If the paper is doing institutional CA in medical, political, therapeutic, legal, or educational settings, there will be a description of the setting and a more detailed summary of the data corpus. For example, in studies using our collection of calls reporting concerns to the U.K. National Society for the Prevention of Cruelty to Children (NSPCC), we documented the legal mandate of the helpline, the annual volume of calls, the advertising material that informed the callers what the helpline was for, and the setup of the call center (including whether call takers worked with a script, how they made notes, and what kinds of action they might take as a consequence of the call).

We described our access and the ethics procedure put in place with callers. We described the size of our corpus and the different lengths of the calls and gave some indications of the types of callers, the problems being reported, and the spread of call takers that we worked with (see, e.g., Hepburn & Potter, 2007). Sometimes these summaries may be supplemented by ethnographic observations of the settings, although these will be used to enrich the analytic sense of what is going on rather than supplement it; it is an aid to doing analysis rather than the upshot of analysis, which is why it is typically in Methods and Materials rather than Analysis.

RESULTS OR ANALYSIS SECTION

A CA paper is typically organized around a series of conversational extracts. Depending on the journal, this will be in a single Results or Analysis section, or it may simply be sections organized under orderly topic headings. Some phenomena are best documented by many short extracts. Thus, a recent paper on the delicate organization of sniffing in talk (Hoey, 2020) has 18 examples; another on how U.S. police initiate conversation when they stop motorists (Kidwell, 2018) has 37. Where the phenomena are more complex or extended (e.g., giving voice to the thoughts of a nonpresent person with intellectual disabilities—Webb et al., 2018; or troubles arising in the closure of interviews with children about alleged sexual offenses—Childs & Walsh, 2018), there will be fewer, maybe seven or eight, but longer with necessarily more extended analytic discussion of each.

In some cases, all the extracts will be from a single interaction. Schegloff (1999) used the study of the interaction that happens when a psychiatrist assesses a stroke patient for "pragmatic deficit" to show how despite interactional difficulties, the patient also shows subtle pragmatic sophistication. Whalen and colleagues (1988) studied the unfolding of a single emergency call that went wrong when issues of politeness and confusion about dispatch contributed to the death of the caller. Both papers made broader arguments based on intensive studies of single cases (Schegloff, 1987).

If the practices that are the focus of study happen face to face or involve visual or textual displays of some kind, then anonymized visualizations are often included (anonymized stills or line drawings). These might highlight interactionally relevant features of eye gaze, gesture, or physical setups of different kinds. These are necessarily used sparingly because journal space is restricted. Sometimes it will be possible to have more extended material made available through a web link. Typically, researchers are balancing needs for anonymity, a desire to provide rich access to the data, the space constraints of the journal, and the resources required for web support.

High-resolution video stills aid the reader's ability to see eye gaze, gesture, and embodied aspects of the setting but at the expense of making participants easily identifiable. The art is to use video and image software that anonymizes sufficiently to disguise the speakers without losing the analytically important information about gaze and gesture. Sharing data through websites can help enrich the analysis by providing further examples for inspection and allowing readers to hear the original talk but can also generate more challenges for sustaining compliance with institutional review board protocols. And web resources of this kind can be expensive for journals to maintain and can provide an extra burden for research groups to support. This is an issue that journal editors and publishers continue to grapple with.

Increasingly, CA researchers are working with materials in languages other than English. As documented in Hepburn and Bolden (2017), this will involve extra space to capture the translation and the role of varied syntax; for example, the placement of the verb in a turn will have consequences for when precisely the recipient is able to project what the action will be. Lay speakers have extremely highly developed skills at such projection; the materials reproduced in articles must allow readers to see properly how they are using those skills.

Where the analysis works with material from institutional settings, it will often be important to cross-refer to other institutions so that the distinctive institutional fingerprint can be captured. Thus, in our study of how calls to a U.K. child protection helpline were opened, we highlighted how they were different from the openings of 911 calls to the emergency services. Instead of launching directly into the reason for the call, callers commonly use a construction such as "I'm a bit concerned," which works as a platform for a collaborative unpacking of a report of possible abuse (Potter & Hepburn, 2003). The practices we see in each institutional setting are finely tuned to the different needs of each service.

Whatever else is in the analytic section, it is fundamental that the claims about each and all extracts can stand up to scrutiny. As set out in Chapter 3, conversational extracts are presented with line numbers so claims can be precisely tied to specific elements of the extract. Usually, by the time it gets into a paper, an extract will have been listened to or watched many times—researchers will have considered alternative explanations; it may have been the topic of a data session where other analysts tested the claims. The precision of the analysis is a consequence of this intensive focus and the need to link each element of the claim to specific features (words, intonation, timing, structure, and so on) of the extract.

In the process of refereeing, claims may be contested, with alternative accounts for what is going on suggested. High-quality refereeing is a community duty that has been important for the development of the field; it sets the high standard for analysis against which CA should be tested. And even when a CA paper is published, it is open to future analysts to contest the claims or offer further claims that may build on or undercut the originals.

DISCUSSION AND CONCLUSION SECTION

CA researchers typically end papers with a summary of findings, providing a pithy description of the practice that has been identified. For example, our article on NSPCC callers' use of concern formats at the start of calls summarizes five separate features of such constructions and considers the role of each in the child protection work of the helpline (Potter & Hepburn, 2003). This description situates the findings in the context of the broader CA literature and summarizes the implications for the psychological literature; it may also highlight the implications for training or organizational practice.

TIPS FOR APPLYING THE TOOLS IN THIS CHAPTER

When researchers start writing up CA, they often include too many observations about each data extract, with the observations made in extract line order. Working with tips for synthesizing analysis in the final section of Chapter 5, create an outline of the extracts that best support your argument. The art is to highlight precisely what is relevant to the identification of the focal practice, action, and so forth, and show that alternative accounts of what is going on are not viable—and no more than that. Take Emmanuel Schegloff's (1992) paper on repair that comes late and what it means for conversation and intersubjectivity or John Heritage and Geoff Raymond's (2005) paper on the subtle ways that epistemic alignment is managed in conversation. Both repay repeated readings for the precision and subtlety of their analysis and the way they bring different examples together to build an argument to a powerful conclusion. Rereading each and tracing the claims to specific lines, lexical items, and responses is a master class in CA. Both are listed in the Appendix as exemplar studies.

Where possible, a way for beginners to succeed in writing CA papers is to collaborate with a trained conversation analyst. This goes for both learning CA and for writing CA papers.

SUMMARY

This chapter has set out a range of considerations that need to be weighed when making judgments about what should be included at various points throughout the writing process. The type of data you have impacts on both the analysis and on how much detail the reader will need to understand the action, practices, and/or specialized activities that you describe. The key here is providing readers with rich access to your data and clearly connecting each analytic claim to individual extracts and the pattern across extracts. When providing context and choosing extracts to present, you will need to attend to the type of journal—its disciplinary focus, its readership, and its space limitations.

7 METHODOLOGICAL INTEGRITY

Methodological integrity is at the heart of conversation analytic work. In his paper on integrity, Emmanuel Schegloff (2005) argued that conversation analysis (CA) is precisely designed to reveal the nature of conversation as a central part of a distinct interaction order. Put simply, if you want to study talk-in-interaction specifically, then CA is designed to be the best method to use. It contrasts with the different methods that try to quickly move beyond the interaction order to underlying cognitive or neurological entities. This may seem obvious, but it has consequential implications. Psychologists should not expect to use CA to study notions developed with the common methods and theories of psychology without theoretical consequence.

For instance, you should not expect to use CA as yet another method with which to study attitudes, to sit alongside questions using Likert scales, say. This is because attitudes as a research object have been formed within the cognitivist logic of psychology, and their study has evolved using certain standardized measures and experiments. If we start to address "attitudes" in CA terms, we will need to understand how assessment appears in conversation. This will involve considering how assessments are organized into adjacency pairs (as we saw in Chapter 5). We can then consider how

https://doi.org/10.1037/0000251-007
Essentials of Conversation Analysis, by A. Hepburn and J. Potter
Copyright © 2021 by the American Psychological Association. All rights reserved.

assessments can be built as objective features of the world or, alternatively, how they can be avowed as something more like individual attitudes (Edwards & Potter, 2017). This will open up new questions, such as why speakers sometimes do both objective and individual together (Potter et al., 2020). The point, then, is that we should not expect that there will be a simple one-to-one relationship between a concept developed within psychological theorizing and an interactional phenomenon that is live for participants. Although CA is profoundly relevant to social and psychological issues, such issues are understood with a focus on their integrity in and for interaction (Potter & Edwards, 2013).

FOUNDATIONAL ISSUES

We structure this chapter around the important issues for the conduct and reporting of qualitative work, using Levitt et al. (2017) as a template. Levitt et al. highlighted three general issues: narrative, transparency, and contextualization. These general issues helped refine our discussion in Chapter 1 of where CA sits with respect to other qualitative approaches, as well as psychological approaches more broadly.

Narrative

Levitt et al. (2017) noted that qualitative papers are often organized in first-person *narrative* form, telling the story of how the materials were analyzed and the conclusions arrived at. With one or two notable exceptions, CA papers are not organized in this way. They are not trying to tell the story of how the researcher came to a realization; rather, they organize carefully transcribed data examples to support a case for a particular claim about an interactional practice of some kind. The focus is on making the relationship between data and claim as clear as possible; the unfolding realizations and false starts of the researcher may be biographically interesting but are not germane to the adequacy of those claims.

Transparency

CA papers have a strong focus on *transparency*. However, this transparency is not seen as coming from the researcher speculating on their own biography and values (the relationship of such descriptions to research claims is itself an interesting area of study for researchers interested in the role of descriptions and epistemics; Potter, 2020). Rather, the transparency comes from making the analytic operations available to inspection, putting readers in the position where they can audit claims. CA claims are not warranted by the researcher telling you that the process of research has led them to a truth, which readers must take on trust. Instead, they are warranted through the application of CA tools and concepts to carefully transcribed data, with claims publicly and carefully tied to specific features of data extracts, which are open for audit by referees and readers.

Contextualization

Contextualization is a central theme within CA, although it has been addressed in ways that differ from many, perhaps most, other approaches. First, CA highlights the sequential context of talk. This is not merely a methodological preference; 50 years of cumulative research since the original Sacks and colleagues (1974) paper has highlighted the consequentiality of sequential positioning for understanding any action (see Clift, 2016, for an integrative summary of the CA literature). This attention to sequence differs markedly from the still-common qualitative research practice (in psychology and elsewhere), where extracts from open-ended interview answers are quoted without reproducing either the question that prompted them or the full turn from which they are lifted (Silverman, 2017). Second, conversation analysts focus on the institutional context of talk. Their work has highlighted the significance of different institutional contexts and also offers a way of analyzing those different contexts. Third, conversation analysts treat context as an issue that participants themselves have to manage: Has the lesson started? Is she a girl or a woman? Varied contextual particulars are continually brought into talk, invoked, alluded to, oriented to, and denied. Rather than needing an ethnographer to tell speakers which culture or category or identity is relevant, this is displayed and worked out locally. In this sense, conversation constantly provides its own updated ethnography. Context is a complex issue, and Schegloff (1997), in an illuminating and influential debate with Billig (1999) and Wetherell (1998), highlighted the telling CA questions: Whose text? Whose context?

CATEGORIZING CONVERSATION ANALYSIS AS A METHOD

Levitt et al. (2017) offered a useful grid in which to situate research methods so they can be compared with one another. We will follow this in our overview.

Approach to Inquiry

What philosophical assumptions do conversation analysts make? It is important to recognize that CA did not arise out of philosophical analysis. Conversation analysts are strongly empiricist and descriptive, with their focus on carefully transcribed audio and video materials. Such work requires the high degree of precision needed to capture what is live and relevant for participants. As we showed earlier, fractions of a second can be crucial for how a turn of talk is understood. Conversation analysts have continually honed their empirical precision as the relevance of more features of talk becomes clear. CA is also noncognitivist—that is, its goal is not to explain practices by way of supposedly independent reference to thoughts, beliefs, or intentions.

Data Collection Strategies

CA works almost exclusively with audio and video records of natural interaction. Where natural interaction draws on texts (e.g., psychiatric reports, legal briefs), it may consider how these are invoked in situ. Where natural interaction involves the use of display screens (e.g., air traffic control rooms), records of what can be seen by participants should be collected. Where interaction is mediated through some virtual media (Facebook Messenger, Zoom), the particular timings and affordances of the medium will need to be included (Meredith, 2021).

Data Analytic Strategies

Conversation analysts use the tools detailed in a wide range of cumulative CA studies to elucidate the role of conversational practices in the context of sequences in particular settings. Crucially, attention to participants' displayed orientations grounds the analysis in the materials. CA researchers celebrate the precision and specificity that this allows compared with strategies that use secondary data (e.g., participants' post hoc accounts of what they did or thought, and why) decomposed into themes or grounded theories.

Research Design

The approach, data collection strategies, and data analytic strategies come together in CA's overall research design. It is quite distinct from other research approaches. In terms of its trustworthiness, the audit trail for CA claims is explicit—the findings can be assessed by any competent reader, and one of its notable features is that it is reproducible. Once a phenomenon has been identified, it can be searched for in new material, and it can form the basis of student exercises and new studies. Fidelity to subject matter is foundational to CA. A large part of the research time in CA is precisely developing and refining analysis, testing against new examples, and considering alternative possibilities.

UTILITY IN ACHIEVING RESEARCH GOALS

Levitt et al. (2017) highlighted four elements needed to achieve research goals. Again, we situate CA in terms of these.

Contextualization of Data

As noted earlier, conversation analysts have a profound, nuanced, and distinctive take on contextualizing data. Take cultural context, for example. An analysis of repair in bilingual immigrant communities can highlight the role of different expertise in brokering understanding and how this unfolds collaboratively (Bolden, 2012). Or take television news interviews: CA work has shown how both interviewers and interviewees manage their talk in a way that displays an orientation to the institutional requirements of this context (Clayman & Heritage, 2002).

Catalyst for Insight

Conversation analysts start with data that provides rich grounds for insightful analysis. They collect material to let the world in and see how it works rather than starting with preformulated themes from psychological or social theory. Commonly, conversation analysts will start research by engaging a rich collection of materials using a process of "unmotivated looking." This is designed to throw up ideas and questions that are often outside the standard social research narratives.

Meaningful Contributions

A key analytic aim is to generate findings that address the analytic goals. Analytic integrity of this kind is foundational to CA. A high proportion of the research time expended by conversation analysts is focused on analysis (as opposed to data collection, theorizing, design).

Coherence Among Findings

A notable feature of CA is that years of accumulation of research studies provides a secure platform for further research. Where disparities between studies have been found, this can be a pathway to revealing cultural or institutional differences. Coherence with earlier work is a major way of showing the validity of an analysis.

Overall, CA is a naturalistic perspective on interaction that can throw light on psychological issues by starting with records of people living their lives in families, workplaces, and professional settings. CA, therefore, more than satisfies the tests of methodological integrity set by Levitt et al. (2017).

SUMMARY

Methodological integrity is central to CA as an approach to conversation as a central part of the interaction order. CA has a high degree of transparency; readers are able to compare specific claims with data examples. CA is contextual, with its focus on understanding the sequential position of practices and their institutional context. Fidelity to subject matter is paramount.

8 SUMMARY AND CONCLUSIONS

Conversation analysis (CA) is designed to reveal how interaction works in both everyday and more specialized settings. Analysts may identify particular interactional practices (turn initial address terms) or social actions (making invitations, complaining, assessing), and they may show how such actions and practices work in the service of institutional tasks (advice giving, counseling, soothing, reporting). Conversation analysts work directly with records of interaction happening independently of the researcher, avoiding secondary data generation, such as interviews and surveys, and avoiding the glosses produced in ethnographic description. In principle, the data should always allow the researcher to work back to the situated interaction; in CA, it has not been transformed into themes or counts. CA papers have extracts from extended stretches of interaction, and analysis will often return to the raw material; referees of CA studies can and do ask for more data or more context for data extracts or more detail on prosody or setting.

There is much work on core human activities—greeting, requesting, offering, accusing, assessing, laughing, crying, admonishing, complimenting, storytelling, threatening, empathizing. There is a complementary body of work on interaction in legal, medical, clinical, educational, and organizational

https://doi.org/10.1037/0000251-008
Essentials of Conversation Analysis, by A. Hepburn and J. Potter

settings focused on showing how primary care is organized, how health visitors advise new mothers, how cancer patients are supported in the move from treatment to palliative care, and how suicides are talked out of self-harm in crisis negotiation.

There is now a well-established set of tools, identified through a cumulative set of studies over 5 decades, that can help us work with any fresh data set. The main parts of Chapters 4 and 5 were overviews of the core set of tools that researchers commonly deploy to start systematic analysis.

BENEFITS

Emmanuel Schegloff (1991) suggested that the "primordial scene of social life is that of direct interaction between members of a social species" (p. 154). CA gets closer to that scene, capturing more of its ordering and complexity than any other approach. CA is rigorous and generative. Claims can be replicated—once a practice is identified, researchers are able to identify that same practice in new settings or study the way it is modified or extended to do institutional work. CA offers a different way to study cultural difference and cultural change: We can consider how practices appear different, or even not at all, in different cultural settings. Or we can see how the same interactional task is done by different practices. All of this work puts the analytic claims, and their basis in data, absolutely at the center of our projects. Conversation analysts offer their claims for rigorous audit in a way that few other approaches are able to.

Some researchers adopt qualitative methods because of an interest in humanity and experience, and maybe feelings, and consequently, may suppose that the technical features of CA stand in the way of that. However, this is not our experience of doing analyses. When we work with this approach, we find that it captures the subtlety of how people interact with one another and the enormous delicacy with which they adjust their behavior, moment by moment, and the exquisite attentiveness to one another that is central to human life. We can study a phone call between two adult sisters, where declining an invitation moves in an oblique and moving way into upset caused by a failed marriage, all of which is played out in indirect description, delays, tiny pieces of tremulous delivery, and carefully calibrated sympathy and empathy (Hepburn & Potter, 2012). This is the core stuff of humanity—CA puts life under scrutiny in a way that foregrounds the perspectives and understandings of the participants. The technicality does not replace the humanity.

CA was not founded as an applied discipline designed to support interventions. However, researchers have increasingly been using it to tackle practical issues. Primary care medicine is one arena where conversation analysts have addressed applied questions. For example, there is a well-established and troubling overprescription of antibiotics to children with adhesive otitis ("glue ear") in the United States. CA studies have found that one way physicians can effectively head off this unnecessary prescription is to deliver online commentary that describes what the physician is seeing, thinking, or feeling during the physical examination ("I don't see anything in that ear") and, therefore, gives some access to their diagnostic reasoning. Such commentary can foreshadow the absence of need for antibiotics and reduce parents' pursuit of inappropriate prescriptions (Robinson & Heritage, 2014).

Another area of impact is through improving the training of professionals working in different settings. One of the features of CA is that analysis stays close to the original interaction. Workshops can provide an environment for bringing together professionals with high-level members' skills and analysts who have built a research-based understanding of the professional work. Such workshops can allow already skilled professionals to crystallize their understanding of their practices so they can then use them more strategically. Sometimes such workshops can provide reassurance to professionals who view their practice as messy, perhaps compared with idealizations in training materials or simulated role-play. The workshop can highlight how the apparent mess is a consequence of managing several simultaneous interactional projects (Hepburn et al., 2014; Stokoe, 2014).

LIMITATIONS

Doing CA well, like many other approaches, requires a notable investment of time and effort and mastery and application of technical language and formal transcription conventions to learn and apply effectively. Although the basics can be learned from a book like this, learning to transcribe well takes time and effort. Considerable practice is involved. Applying the tools correctly to new material is a level of difficulty up from understanding them with a brief illustrative example selected to make the point. Again, considerable practice is involved, and that practice is inevitably more successful when there is the support of a skilled conversation analyst. Internationally, training workshops are regularly run for both beginners and advanced analysts to give them a chance to refine their skills and enhance the general pool of competent analysts. There are many in CA, like us, who are committed to supporting this training.

A feature of CA that can be frustrating to psychologists and other social theorists coming to it for the first time is that it is not appropriate for addressing many psychological questions, at least when formulated in the established language of variables and effects, acting on or mediated by cognitive events or processes. Confusion and incoherence will likely arise if psychologists supplement an existing study or blend it into a mixed-methods project. It takes considerable work and some theoretical innovation to rework a psychological issue in CA terms. For example, Derek Edwards (1994) rethought the notion of cognitive scripts by considering practices of script formulation and what those practices do (e.g., make an account for a potentially problematic action by formulating it as standard or regular). He then explored the implications of this formulation for cognitive notions of scripts (Edwards, 1997) and showed how this plays out in couples counseling (Edwards, 1995). We, of course, think CA produces work that is exciting, generative, and rewarding and of great psychological value; indeed, it can completely reconfigure how we think about psychology. But other psychologists might feel that it has taken them away from their core issues.

MOVING FORWARD WITH CONVERSATION ANALYSIS

CA is directly relevant to social, developmental, counseling, organizational, and clinical psychology, where many of the central phenomena are embedded in interaction. For these domains, it has the benefit of supplementing standard quantitative and qualitative methods with work that starts with natural interaction. Moreover, the standard methods in these areas are typically themselves dependent on interaction—administering scales with embedded linguistic constructions, running experiments using prompts and categories, performing open-ended interviews, and so on—and it is interesting and perhaps revealing to apply CA to the very interaction through which research is conducted. It is notable that, in other scientific disciplines, there can be a considerable focus on studying the operation of measurement instruments, and it is perhaps time for psychologists to systematically study the operation of their own instruments.

CA has been particularly effective in revealing practices at work in institutional domains such as health, law, and media. These are areas where psychologists have a range of overlapping interests, and CA work can inform those interests or stimulate new kinds of studies. CA work has a long tradition of considering the way objects, gestures, texts, and screens of different kinds are embedded in action sequences. For example, Christian Heath and colleagues (2018) focused on how different implements and materials are passed efficiently between medical practitioners in the course of surgical operations. In increasingly technically mediated workplaces, CA is able to capture the subtle interaction of text and screen in professional settings. Online communication platforms have different affordances in terms of sequence, timing, text versus voice, absence of prosody, and so on. Meredith (2020) showed how CA offers a systematic framework for studying how actions are accomplished in these special environments.

CA may seem to have less relevance to areas of psychology, such as cognitive or even neuro, but there is a range of potential relevancies that come from work on epistemics or the projectability of actions (see, e.g., Heritage, 2012; Levinson, 2019). Even such physiology-based topics as food taste can be approached from an interactional perspective, highlighting issues of culture, practice, and expertise (Mondada, 2018). Our aim with this book is to provide a platform for psychologists to start to explore the value of CA for their topics. Many possibilities for fruitful interchange and innovation are coming into view. We hope you will find this book a route to something extraordinary.

Appendix

EXEMPLAR STUDIES

Edwards, D. (2005). Moaning, whinging and laughing: The subjective side of complaints. *Discourse Studies, 7*(1), 5–29. https://doi.org/10.1177/1461445605048765

Hepburn, A., & Potter, J. (2007). Crying receipts: Time, empathy, and institutional practice. *Research on Language and Social Interaction, 40*(1), 89–116. https://doi.org/10.1080/08351810701331299

Hepburn, A., & Potter, J. (2011). Threats: Power, family mealtimes, and social influence. *British Journal of Social Psychology, 50*(1), 99–120. https://doi.org/10.1348/014466610X500791

Heritage, J., & Raymond, G. (2005). The terms of agreement: Indexing epistemic authority and subordination in talk-in-interaction. *Social Psychology Quarterly, 68*(1), 15–38. https://doi.org/10.1177/019027250506800103

Heritage, J., & Stivers, T. (1999). Online commentary in acute medical visits: A method of shaping patient expectations. *Social Science & Medicine, 49*(11), 1501–1517. https://doi.org/10.1016/S0277-9536(99)00219-1

Koole, T. (2010). Displays of epistemic access: Student responses to teacher explanations. *Research on Language and Social Interaction, 43*(2), 183–209. https://doi.org/10.1080/08351811003737846

Lerner, G. (1995). Turn design and the organization of participation in instructional activities. *Discourse Processes, 19*(1), 111–131. https://doi.org/10.1080/01638539109544907

Leydon, G. M., Ekberg, K., & Drew, P. (2013). "How can I help?" Nurse call openings on a cancer helpline and implications for call progressivity. *Patient Education and Counseling, 92*(1), 23–30. https://doi.org/10.1016/j.pec.2013.02.007

Pomerantz, A. (1988). Offering a candidate answer: An information seeking strategy. *Communications Monographs, 55*(4), 360–373. https://doi.org/10.1080/03637758809376177

Raymond, G., & Heritage, J. (2006). The epistemics of social relations: Owning grandchildren. *Language in Society, 35*(5), 677–705. https://doi.org/10.1017/S0047404506060325

Robinson, J. D., & Heritage, J. (2014). Intervening with conversation analysis: The case of medicine. *Research on Language and Social Interaction, 47*(3), 201–218. https://doi.org/10.1080/08351813.2014.925658

Schegloff, E. A. (1992). Repair after next turn: The last structurally provided defense of intersubjectivity in conversation. *American Journal of Sociology, 97*(5), 1295–1345. https://doi.org/10.1086/229903

Schegloff, E. A. (1996). Confirming allusions: Toward an empirical account of action. *American Journal of Sociology, 102*(1), 161–216. https://doi.org/10.1086/230911

Schegloff, E. A., & Sacks, H. (1973). Opening up closings. *Semiotica, 8*(4), 289–327. https://doi.org/10.1515/semi.1973.8.4.289

Shaw, C., Chrysikou, V., Davis, S., Gessler, S., Rodin, G., & Lanceley, A. (2017). Inviting end-of-life talk in initial CALM therapy sessions: A conversation analytic study. *Patient Education and Counseling, 100*(2), 259–266. https://doi.org/10.1016/j.pec.2016.08.024

Silverman, D., & Peräkylä, A. (1990). AIDS counselling: The interactional organisation of talk about 'delicate' issues. *Sociology of Health & Illness, 12*(3), 293–318. https://doi.org/10.1111/1467-9566.ep11347251

Stokoe, E. (2010). 'I'm not gonna hit a lady': Conversation analysis, membership categorization and men's denials of violence towards women. *Discourse & Society, 21*(1), 59–82. https://doi.org/10.1177/0957926509345072

Sutherland, O., Peräkylä, A., & Elliott, R. (2014). Conversation analysis of the two-chair self-soothing task in emotion-focused therapy. *Psychotherapy Research, 24*(6), 738–751. https://doi.org/10.1080/10503307.2014.885146

Wilkinson, R. (2014). Intervening with conversation analysis in speech and language therapy: Improving aphasic conversation. *Research on Language and Social Interaction, 47*(3), 219–238. https://doi.org/10.1080/08351813.2014.925659

References

Bales, R. F. (1950). *Interaction process analysis*. Addison-Wesley.

Barker, R. G., & Wright, H. F. (1951). *One boy's day: A specimen record of behavior*. Harper.

Billig, M. (1999). Whose terms? Whose ordinariness? Rhetoric and ideology in conversation analysis. *Discourse & Society, 10*(4), 543–558. https://doi.org/10.1177/0957926599010004005

Bolden, G. B. (2012). Across languages and cultures: Brokering problems of understanding in conversational repair. *Language in Society, 41*(1), 97–121. https://doi.org/10.1017/S0047404511000923

Bolden, G. B., Mandelbaum, J., & Wilkinson, S. (2012). Pursuing a response by repairing an indexical reference. *Research on Language and Social Interaction, 45*(2), 137–155. https://doi.org/10.1080/08351813.2012.673380

Butler, C. W., Potter, J., Danby, S., Emmison, M., & Hepburn, A. (2010). Advice-implicative interrogatives: Building "client-centered" support in a children's helpline. *Social Psychology Quarterly, 73*(3), 265–287. https://doi.org/10.1177/0190272510379838

Childs, C., & Walsh, D. (2018). Paradoxical invitations: Challenges in soliciting more information from child witnesses. *Research on Language and Social Interaction, 51*(4), 363–378. https://doi.org/10.1080/08351813.2018.1524561

Chomsky, N. (2006). *Language and mind* (3rd ed.). Cambridge University Press. https://doi.org/10.1017/CBO9780511791222

Clayman, S. E. (2010). Address terms in the service of other actions: The case of news interview discourse. *Discourse & Communication, 4*(2), 161–183. https://doi.org/10.1177/1750481310364330

Clayman, S. E., & Heritage, J. (2002). Questioning presidents: Journalistic deference and adversarialness in the press conferences of Eisenhower and Reagan. *Journal of Communication, 52*(4), 749–775. https://doi.org/10.1111/j.1460-2466.2002.tb02572.x

Clift, R. (2016). *Conversation analysis*. Cambridge University Press.

Couper-Kuhlen, E., & Selting, M. (Eds.). (1996). *Prosody in conversation: Interactional studies.* Cambridge University Press. https://doi.org/10.1017/CBO9780511597862

Craven, A., & Potter, J. (2010). Directives: Entitlement and contingency in action. *Discourse Studies, 12*(4), 419–442. https://doi.org/10.1177/1461445610370126

Drew, P. (1992). Contested evidence in courtroom cross-examination: The case of a trial for rape. In P. Drew & J. Heritage (Eds.), *Talk at work: Interaction in institutional settings* (pp. 470–520). Cambridge University Press.

Drew, P. (1997). 'Open' class repair initiators in response to sequential sources of troubles in conversation. *Journal of Pragmatics, 28*(1), 69–101. https://doi.org/10.1016/S0378-2166(97)89759-7

Drew, P., & Heritage, J. (1992). Introduction: Analysing talk at work. In P. Drew & J. Heritage (Eds.), *Talk at work* (pp. 3–65). Cambridge University Press.

Edwards, D. (1994). Script formulations: An analysis of event descriptions in conversation. *Journal of Language and Social Psychology, 13*(3), 211–247. https://doi.org/10.1177/0261927X94133001

Edwards, D. (1995). Two to tango: Script formulations, dispositions, and rhetorical symmetry in relationship troubles talk. *Research on Language and Social Interaction, 28*(4), 319–350. https://doi.org/10.1207/s15327973rlsi2804_1

Edwards, D. (1997). *Discourse and cognition.* SAGE.

Edwards, D., & Potter, J. (2017). Some uses of subject-side assessments. *Discourse Studies, 19*(5), 497–514. https://doi.org/10.1177/1461445617715171

Enfield, N. J., Stivers, T., & Levinson, S. C. (2010). Question–response sequences in conversation across ten languages: An introduction. *Journal of Pragmatics, 42*(10), 2615–2619. https://doi.org/10.1016/j.pragma.2010.04.001

Ford, J., Hepburn, A., & Parry, R. (2019). What do displays of empathy do in palliative care consultations? *Discourse Studies, 21*(1), 22–37. https://doi.org/10.1177/1461445618814030

Garfinkel, H. (1967). *Studies in ethnomethodology.* Prentice Hall.

Glenn, P. J., & Holt, E. (Eds.). (2013). *Studies of laughter in interaction.* Bloomsbury. https://doi.org/10.5040/9781472542069

Goffman, E. (1959). *The presentation of self in everyday life.* Penguin.

Golato, A., & Fagyal, Z. (2008). Comparing single and double sayings of the German response token *ja* and the role of prosody: A conversation analytic perspective. *Research on Language and Social Interaction, 41*(3), 241–270. https://doi.org/10.1080/08351810802237834

Heath, C., Luff, P., Sanchez-Svensson, M., & Nicholls, M. (2018). Exchanging implements: The micro-materialities of multidisciplinary work in the operating theatre. *Sociology of Health & Illness, 40*(2), 297–313. https://doi.org/10.1111/1467-9566.12594

Hepburn, A. (2004). Crying: Notes on description, transcription, and interaction. *Research on Language and Social Interaction, 37*(3), 251–290. https://doi.org/10.1207/s15327973rlsi3703_1

Hepburn, A. (2020). The preference for self-direction as a resource for parents' socialisation practices. *Qualitative Research in Psychology, 17*(3), 450–468. https://doi.org/10.1080/14780887.2019.1664679

Hepburn, A., & Bolden, G. B. (2017). *Transcribing for social research.* SAGE. https://doi.org/10.4135/9781473920460

Hepburn, A., & Potter, J. (2004). Discourse analytic practice. In C. Seale, G. Gobo, J. F. Gubrium, & D. Silverman (Eds.), *Qualitative research practice* (pp. 168–185). SAGE. https://doi.org/10.4135/9781848608191.d16

Hepburn, A., & Potter, J. (2007). Crying receipts: Time, empathy, and institutional practice. *Research on Language and Social Interaction, 40*(1), 89–116. https://doi.org/10.1080/08351810701331299

Hepburn, A., & Potter, J. (2011). Threats: Power, family mealtimes, and social influence. *The British Journal of Social Psychology, 50*(1), 99–120. https://doi.org/10.1348/014466610X500791

Hepburn, A., & Potter, J. (2012). Crying and crying responses. In A. Peräkylä & M.-L. Sorjonen (Eds.), *Emotion in interaction* (pp. 195–210). Oxford University Press. https://doi.org/10.1093/acprof:oso/9780199730735.003.0009

Hepburn, A., & Varney, S. (2013). Beyond ((laughter)): Some notes on transcription. In P. J. Glenn & E. Holt (Eds.), *Studies in laughter in interaction* (pp. 25–38). Bloomsbury. https://doi.org/10.5040/9781472542069.ch-002

Hepburn, A., Wilkinson, S., & Butler, C. W. (2014). Intervening with conversation analysis in telephone helpline services: Strategies to improve effectiveness. *Research on Language and Social Interaction, 47*(3), 239–254. https://doi.org/10.1080/08351813.2014.925661

Hepburn, A., Wilkinson, S., & Shaw, R. (2012). Repairing self- and recipient reference. *Research on Language and Social Interaction, 45*(2), 175–190. https://doi.org/10.1080/08351813.2012.673914

Heritage, J. (1984a). A change-of-state token and aspects of its sequential placement. In J. M. Atkinson & J. Heritage (Eds.), *Structures of social action: Studies in conversation analysis* (pp. 299–345). Cambridge University Press.

Heritage, J. (1984b). *Garfinkel and ethnomethodology.* Wiley.

Heritage, J. (1998). Conversation analysis and talk: Analyzing distinctive turn-taking systems. In S. Cmejrkova, J. Hofmanova, O. Mullerova, & J. Svetla (Eds.), *Dialogue analysis* VI (pp. 3–18). Niemeyer. https://doi.org/10.1515/9783110965049-001

Heritage, J. (2010). Conversation analysis: Practices and methods. In D. Silverman (Ed.), *Qualitative sociology* (3rd ed., pp. 208–230). SAGE.

Heritage, J. (2012). Epistemics in action: Action formation and territories of knowledge. *Research on Language and Social Interaction, 45*(1), 1–29. https://doi.org/10.1080/08351813.2012.646684

Heritage, J. (2013). Language and social institutions: The conversation analytic view. *Waiguoyu, 36*(4), 2–27.

Heritage, J., & Clayman, S. (2010). *Talk in action: Interactions, identities, and institutions.* Wiley.

Heritage, J., & Raymond, G. (2005). The terms of agreement: Indexing epistemic authority and subordination in talk-in-interaction. *Social Psychology Quarterly*, *68*(1), 15–38. https://doi.org/10.1177/019027250506800103

Heritage, J., & Stivers, T. (1999). Online commentary in acute medical visits: A method of shaping patient expectations. *Social Science & Medicine, 49*(11), 1501–1517. https://doi.org/10.1016/S0277-9536(99)00219-1

Hoey, E. M. (2020). Waiting to inhale: On sniffing in conversation. *Research on Language and Social Interaction, 53*(1), 118–139. https://doi.org/10.1080/08351813.2020.1712962

Jefferson, G. (1978a). Explanation of transcript notation. In J. Schenken (Ed.), *Studies in the organization of conversational interaction* (pp. xii–xv). Academic Press.

Jefferson, G. (1978b). Sequential aspects of storytelling in conversation. In J. Schenkein (Ed.), *Studies in the organization of conversational interaction* (pp. 219–248). Academic Press. https://doi.org/10.1016/B978-0-12-623550-0.50016-1

Jefferson, G. (1984). On the organization of laughter in talk about troubles. In J. M. Atkinson & J. Heritage (Eds.), *Structures of social action* (pp. 346–369). Cambridge University Press.

Kevoe-Feldman, H., & Pomerantz, A. (2018). Critical timing of actions for transferring 911 calls in a wireless call center. *Discourse Studies, 20*(4), 488–505. https://doi.org/10.1177/1461445618756182

Kidwell, M. (2018). Early alignment in police traffic stops. *Research on Language and Social Interaction, 51*(3), 292–312. https://doi.org/10.1080/08351813.2018.1485232

Kitzinger, C., & Rickford, R. (2007). VI. Becoming a 'bloke': The construction of gender in interaction. *Feminism & Psychology, 17*(2), 214–223. https://doi.org/10.1177/0959353507076554

Kitzinger, C., Shaw, R., & Toerien, M. (2012). Referring to persons without using a full-form reference: Locally initial indexicals in action. *Research on Language and Social Interaction, 45*(2), 116–136. https://doi.org/10.1080/08351813.2012.673376

Lerner, G. H. (1992). Assisted storytelling: Deploying shared knowledge as a practical matter. *Qualitative Sociology, 15*(3), 247–271. https://doi.org/10.1007/BF00990328

Lerner, G. H. (1996). Finding "face" in the preference structures of talk-in-interaction. *Social Psychology Quarterly, 59*(4), 303–321. https://doi.org/10.2307/2787073

Levinson, S. C. (2013). Action formation and ascription. In J. Sidnell & T. Stivers (Eds.), *The handbook of conversation analysis* (pp. 101–130). Blackwell.

Levinson, S. C. (2019). Interactional foundations of language: The interaction engine hypothesis. In P. Hagoort (Ed.), *Human language: From genes and brain to behavior* (pp. 189–200). MIT Press.

Levitt, H. M., Motulsky, S. L., Wertz, F. J., Morrow, S. L., & Ponterotto, J. G. (2017). Recommendations for designing and reviewing qualitative research in psychology: Promoting methodological integrity. *Qualitative Psychology, 4*(1), 2–22. https://doi.org/10.1037/qup0000082

Local, J. (1996). Conversational phonetics: Some aspects of news receipts in everyday talk. In E. Couper-Kuhlen & M. Selting (Eds.), *Prosody in conversation: Interactional studies* (Studies in Interactional Sociolinguistics, pp. 177–230). Cambridge University Press. https://doi.org/10.1017/CBO9780511597862.007

Mandelbaum, J. (2013). Storytelling in conversation. In J. Sidnell & T. Stivers (Eds.), *The handbook of conversation analysis* (pp. 492–508). Wiley-Blackwell.

Maynard, D. W. (1997). The news delivery sequence: Bad news and good news in conversational interaction. *Research on Language and Social Interaction, 30*(2), 93–130. https://doi.org/10.1207/s15327973rlsi3002_1

Meredith, J. (2020). Conversation analysis, cyberpsychology and online interaction. *Social and Personality Psychology Compass, 14*(5), 285–294. https://doi.org/10.1111/spc3.12529

Meredith, J. (2021). Using conversation analysis and discursive psychology to analyse online data. In D. Silverman (Ed.), *Qualitative research* (5th ed., pp. 245–262). SAGE.

Mikesell, L., Bolden, G. B., Mandelbaum, J., Robinson, J. D., Romaniuk, T., Bolaños-Carpio, A., Searles, D., Wei, W., DiDomenico, S. M., & Angell, B. (2017). At the intersection of epistemics and action: Responding with *I know*. *Research on Language and Social Interaction, 50*(3), 268–285. https://doi.org/10.1080/08351813.2017.1340711

Mondada, L. (2011). The organization of concurrent courses of action in surgical demonstrations. In J. Streeck, C. Goodwin, & C. LeBaron (Eds.), *Multimodality in communication* (pp. 207–226). Cambridge University Press.

Mondada, L. (2013). The conversation analytic approach to data collection. In J. Sidnell & T. Stivers (Eds.), *The handbook of conversation analysis* (pp. 32–56). Blackwell.

Mondada, L. (2018). The multimodal interactional organization of tasting: Practices of tasting cheese in gourmet shops. *Discourse Studies, 20*(6), 743–769. https://doi.org/10.1177/1461445618793439

Peräkylä, A., & Sorjonen, M. L. (2012). *Emotion in interaction*. Oxford University Press. https://doi.org/10.1093/acprof:oso/9780199730735.001.0001

Pillet-Shore, D. (2012). The problems with praise in parent–teacher interaction. *Communication Monographs, 79*(2), 181–204. https://doi.org/10.1080/03637751.2012.672998

Pomerantz, A. (1980). Telling my side: "Limited access" as a "fishing" device. *Sociological Inquiry, 50*(3–4), 186–198. https://doi.org/10.1111/j.1475-682X.1980.tb00020.x

Pomerantz, A. (1984). Agreeing and disagreeing with assessments: Some features of preferred/dispreferred turn shapes. In J. M. Atkinson & J. C. Heritage (Eds.), *Structures of social action* (pp. 57–101). Cambridge University Press.

Pomerantz, A., & Heritage, J. (2013). Preference. In J. Sidnell & T. Stivers (Eds.), *Handbook of conversation analysis* (pp. 210–228). Cambridge University Press.

Potter, J. (2020). Discursive psychology: A non-cognitivist approach to practices of knowing. In K. Krippendorff & N. I. Halabi (Eds.), *Discourses in action: What language enables us to do* (pp. 71–86). Routledge. https://doi.org/10.4324/9780429356032-4

Potter, J. (2021). Discursive psychology: Capturing the psychological world as it unfolds. In P. M. Camic (Ed.), *Qualitative research in psychology: Expanding perspectives in methodology and design* (2nd ed., pp. 123–145). American Psychological Association. https://doi.org/10.1037/0000252-007

Potter, J., & Edwards, D. (2013). Conversation analysis and psychology. In J. Sidnell & T. Stivers (Eds.), *The handbook of conversation analysis* (pp. 701–725). Blackwell.

Potter, J., & Hepburn, A. (2003). "I'm a bit concerned"—Early actions and psychological constructions in a child protection helpline. *Research on Language and Social Interaction, 36*(3), 197–240. https://doi.org/10.1207/S15327973RLSI3603_01

Potter, J., & Hepburn, A. (2005). Qualitative interviews in psychology: Problems and possibilities. *Qualitative Research in Psychology, 2*(4), 281–307. https://doi.org/10.1191/1478088705qp045oa

Potter, J., Hepburn, A., & Edwards, D. (2020). Rethinking attitudes and social psychology—issues of function, order and combination in subject-side and object-side assessments in natural settings. *Qualitative Research in Psychology, 17*(3), 336–356. https://doi.org/10.1080/14780887.2020.1725952

Potter, J., & Shaw, C. (2018). The virtues of naturalistic data. In U. Flick (Ed.), *The SAGE handbook of qualitative data collection* (pp. 182–199). SAGE. https://doi.org/10.4135/9781526416070.n12

Potter, J., & Wetherell, M. (1987). *Discourse and social psychology: Beyond attitudes and behaviour.* SAGE.

Raymond, G. (2003). Grammar and social organization: Yes/no interrogatives and the structure of responding. *American Sociological Review, 68*(6), 939–967. https://doi.org/10.2307/1519752

Robinson, J. D. (2006). Managing trouble responsibility and relationships during conversational repair. *Communication Monographs, 73*(2), 137–161. https://doi.org/10.1080/03637750600581206

Robinson, J. D., & Heritage, J. (2014). Intervening with conversation analysis: The case of medicine. *Research on Language and Social Interaction, 47*(3), 201–218. https://doi.org/10.1080/08351813.2014.925658

Ruusuvuori, J. (2013). Emotion, affect and conversation. In J. Sidnell & T. Stivers (Eds.), *The handbook of conversation analysis* (pp. 330–349). Wiley-Blackwell.

Sacks, H. (1972). On the analyzability of stories by children. In J. J. Gumperz & D. Hymes (Eds.), *Directions in sociolinguistics: The ethnography of communication* (pp. 325–345). Holt, Rinehart and Winston.

Sacks, H. (1984). Notes on methodology. In J. M. Atkinson & J. Heritage (Eds.), *Structures of social action: Studies in conversation analysis* (pp. 21–27). Cambridge University Press.

Sacks, H. (1987). On the preferences for agreement and contiguity in sequences in conversation. In G. Button & J. R. Lee (Eds.), *Talk and social organisation* (pp. 54–69). Multilingual Matters.

Sacks, H. (1992). *Lectures on conversation* [1964–1972]. Blackwell.

Sacks, H., & Schegloff, E. A. (1979). Two preferences in the organization of reference to persons in conversation and their interaction. In G. Psathas (Ed.), *Everyday language: Studies in ethnomethodology* (pp. 14–21). Irvington.

Sacks, H., Schegloff, E. A., & Jefferson, G. (1974). A simplest systematics for the organization of turn-taking for conversation. *Language, 50*(4), 696–735. https://doi.org/10.1353/lan.1974.0010

Schegloff, E. A. (1968). Sequencing in conversational openings. *American Anthropologist, 70*(6), 1075–1095. https://doi.org/10.1525/aa.1968.70.6.02a00030

Schegloff, E. A. (1987). Analyzing single episodes of interaction: An exercise in conversation analysis. *Social Psychology Quarterly, 50*(2), 101–114. https://doi.org/10.2307/2786745

Schegloff, E. A. (1988). Goffman and the analysis of conversation. In P. Drew & A. Wootton (Eds.), *Erving Goffman: Exploring the interaction order* (pp. 89–135). Polity.

Schegloff, E. A. (1991). Conversation analysis and socially shared cognition. In L. B. Resnick, J. M. Levine, & S. D. Teasley (Eds.), *Perspectives on socially shared cognition* (pp. 150–171). American Psychological Association.

Schegloff, E. A. (1992). Repair after next turn: The last structurally provided defense of intersubjectivity in conversation. *American Journal of Sociology, 97*(5), 1295–1345. https://doi.org/10.1086/229903

Schegloff, E. A. (1993). Reflections on quantification in the study of conversation. *Research on Language and Social Interaction, 26*(1), 99–128. https://doi.org/10.1207/s15327973rlsi2601_5

Schegloff, E. A. (1996). Some practices for referring to persons in talk-in-interaction: A partial sketch of a systematics. In B. A. Fox (Ed.), *Studies in anaphora* [Typological Studies in Language, *33*] (pp. 437–486). John Benjamins Publishing Company.

Schegloff, E. A. (1997). Whose text? Whose context? *Discourse & Society, 8*(2), 165–187. https://doi.org/10.1177/0957926597008002002

Schegloff, E. A. (1998). Reflections on studying prosody in talk-in-interaction. *Language and Speech, 41*(3–4), 235–263. https://doi.org/10.1177/002383099804100402

Schegloff, E. A. (1999). Discourse, pragmatics, conversation, analysis. *Discourse Studies, 1*(4), 405–435. https://doi.org/10.1177/1461445699001004002

Schegloff, E. A. (2005). On integrity in inquiry . . . of the investigated, not the investigator. *Discourse Studies, 7*(4–5), 455–480. https://doi.org/10.1177/1461445605054402

Schegloff, E. A. (2007a). Categories in action: Person-reference and membership categorization. *Discourse Studies, 9*(4), 433–461. https://doi.org/10.1177/1461445607079162

Schegloff, E. A. (2007b). *Sequence organization in interaction: A primer in conversation analysis I*. Cambridge University Press. https://doi.org/10.1017/CBO9780511791208

Schegloff, E. A. (2007c). A tutorial on membership categorization. *Journal of Pragmatics, 39*(3), 462–482. https://doi.org/10.1016/j.pragma.2006.07.007

Schegloff, E. A. (2013). Ten operations in self-initiated, same turn repair. In M. Hayashi, G. Raymond, & J. Sidnell (Eds.), *Conversational repair and human understanding* (pp. 41–70). Cambridge University Press.

Schegloff, E. A., Jefferson, G., & Sacks, H. (1977). The preference for self-correction in the organization of repair in conversation. *Language, 53*(2), 361–382. https://doi.org/10.1353/lan.1977.0041

Schegloff, E. A., & Sacks, H. (1973). Opening up closings. *Semiotica, 8*(4), 289–327. https://doi.org/10.1515/semi.1973.8.4.289

Sidnell, J., & Stivers, T. (Eds.). (2013). *The handbook of conversation analysis*. Wiley.

Sikveland, R., & Stokoe, E. (2016). Dealing with resistance in initial intake and inquiry calls to mediation: The power of "willing." *Conflict Resolution Quarterly, 33*(3), 235–254. https://doi.org/10.1002/crq.21157

Silverman, D. (2017). How was it for you? The Interview Society and the irresistible rise of the (poorly analyzed) interview. *Qualitative Research, 17*(2), 144–158. https://doi.org/10.1177/1468794116668231

Speer, S., & Stokoe, E. (Eds.). (2012). *Conversation and gender*. Cambridge University Press.

Stevanovic, M., Himberg, T., Niinisalo, M., Kahri, M., Peräkylä, A., Sams, M., & Hari, R. (2017). Sequentiality, mutual visibility, and behavioral matching: Body sway and pitch register during joint decision making. *Research on Language and Social Interaction, 50*(1), 33–53. https://doi.org/10.1080/08351813.2017.1262130

Stivers, T., Enfield, N. J., Brown, P., Englert, C., Hayashi, M., Heinemann, T., Hoymann, G., Rossano, F., de Ruiter, J. P., Yoon, K. E., & Levinson, S. C. (2009). Universals and cultural variation in turn-taking in conversation. *Proceedings of the National Academy of Sciences of the United States of America, 106*(26), 10587–10592. https://doi.org/10.1073/pnas.0903616106

Stivers, T., & Rossano, F. (2010). Mobilizing response. *Research on Language and Social Interaction, 43*(1), 3–31. https://doi.org/10.1080/08351810903471258

Stokoe, E. (2014). The Conversation Analytic Role-play Method (CARM): A method for training communication skills as an alternative to simulated role-play. *Research on Language and Social Interaction, 47*(3), 255–265. https://doi.org/10.1080/08351813.2014.925663

te Molder, H., & Potter, J. (Eds.). (2005). *Conversation and cognition*. Cambridge University Press. https://doi.org/10.1017/CBO9780511489990

Voutilainen, L., Peräkylä, A., & Ruusuvuori, J. (2010). Recognition and interpretation: Responding to emotional experience in psychotherapy. *Research on Language and Social Interaction, 43*(1), 85–107. https://doi.org/10.1080/08351810903474799

Waring, H. Z. (2014). Turn allocation and context: Broadening participation in the second language classroom. In J. Flowerdew (Ed.), *Discourse in context: Contemporary applied linguistics* (Vol. 3, pp. 301–320). Bloomsbury.

Webb, J. C., Pilnick, A., & Clegg, J. (2018). Imagined constructed thought: How staff interpret the behavior of patients with intellectual disabilities. *Research on Language and Social Interaction, 51*(4), 347–362. https://doi.org/10.1080/08351813.2018.1523893

Wetherell, M. (1998). Positioning and interpretative repertoires: Conversation analysis and post-structuralism in dialogue. *Discourse & Society, 9*(3), 387–412. https://doi.org/10.1177/0957926598009003005

Whalen, J., & Zimmerman, D. H. (1998). Observations on the display and management of emotion in naturally occurring activities: The case of "hysteria" in calls to 9-1-1. *Social Psychology Quarterly, 61*(2), 141–159. https://doi.org/10.2307/2787066

Whalen, J., Zimmerman, D. H., & Whalen, M. R. (1988). When words fail: A single case analysis. *Social Problems, 35*(4), 335–362. https://doi.org/10.2307/800591

Whitehead, K. A., & Lerner, G. H. (2009). When are persons 'white'?: On some practical asymmetries of racial reference in talk-in-interaction. *Discourse & Society, 20*(5), 613–641. https://doi.org/10.1177/0957926509106413

Wilkinson, S., & Kitzinger, C. (2006). Surprise as an interactional achievement: Reaction tokens in conversation. *Social Psychology Quarterly, 69*(2), 150–182. https://doi.org/10.1177/019027250606900203

Wittgenstein, L. (1953). *Philosophical investigation* (G. E. M. Anscombe, Trans.). Blackwell.

Index

About the Authors

Alexa Hepburn, PhD, is a research professor in the School of Communication and Information at Rutgers University and an honorary professor in the School of Social Science at Loughborough University. She has published widely regarding methodological, practical, theoretical, and metatheoretical frameworks in the social sciences and on the use and development of conversation analytic methods, particularly with regard to emotional expressions such as upset, anger and laughter, parents' strategies for managing children's behavior, techniques for giving advice, and practitioners' empathic responses in clinical encounters. A major focus is to develop new insights into profound issues related to emotion, socialization, and influence and to develop innovative and effective applied research techniques for interaction research. This is reflected in her three books: *An Introduction to Critical Social Psychology, Discursive Research in Practice: New Approaches to Psychology and Interaction,* and her latest coauthored book, *Transcribing for Social Research.* She has delivered over 40 invited seminars, plenaries, and keynotes and over 30 specialist workshops on interaction analysis in 12 different countries around the world. Dr. Hepburn is currently working closely with video materials of family mealtimes and clinical encounters, as well as various types of telephone interaction.

Jonathan Potter, DPhil, is Distinguished Professor and dean of the School of Communication and Information at Rutgers University. He has worked on basic theoretical and methodological issues in social science for more than 40 years. He has engaged with, and developed, poststructuralism (in *Social Texts and Context,* 1984, with Margaret Wetherell and Peter Stringer), discourse analysis (in *Discourse and Social Psychology,* 1987, with Margaret Wetherell), discursive approaches to racism (in *Mapping the Language of*

Racism, 1992, with Margaret Wetherell), discursive psychology (in *Discursive Psychology*, 1992, with Derek Edwards), and constructionism (systematically reworked in *Representing Reality*). He is currently interested in how the conversation analytic method can support a reconfiguration of basic psychological notions, such as attitudes, social influence, and emotions.

About the Series Editors

Clara F. Hill, PhD, earned her doctorate at Southern Illinois University in 1974. She started her career in 1974 as an assistant professor in the Department of Psychology, University of Maryland, College Park, and is currently there as a professor.

She is the president-elect of the Society for the Advancement of Psychotherapy, and has been the president of the Society for Psychotherapy Research, the editor of the *Journal of Counseling Psychology*, and the editor of *Psychotherapy Research*.

Dr. Hill was awarded the Leona Tyler Award for Lifetime Achievement in Counseling Psychology from Division 17 (Society of Counseling Psychology) and the Distinguished Psychologist Award from Division 29 (Society for the Advancement of Psychotherapy) of the American Psychological Association, the Distinguished Research Career Award from the Society for Psychotherapy Research, and the Outstanding Lifetime Achievement Award from the Section on Counseling and Psychotherapy Process and Outcome Research of the Society of Counseling Psychology. Her major research interests are helping skills, psychotherapy process and outcome, training therapists, dream work, and qualitative research.

She has published more than 250 journal articles, 80 chapters in books, and 17 books (including *Therapist Techniques and Client Outcomes: Eight Cases of Brief Psychotherapy*; *Helping Skills: Facilitating Exploration, Insight, and Action*; and *Dream Work in Therapy: Facilitating Exploration, Insight, and Action*).

Sarah Knox, PhD, joined the faculty of Marquette University in 1999 and is a professor in the Department of Counselor Education and Counseling Psychology in the College of Education. She earned her doctorate at the

University of Maryland and completed her predoctoral internship at The Ohio State University.

Dr. Knox's research has been published in a number of journals, including *The Counseling Psychologist, Counselling Psychology Quarterly, Journal of Counseling Psychology, Psychotherapy, Psychotherapy Research,* and *Training and Education in Professional Psychology.* Her publications focus on the psychotherapy process and relationship, supervision and training, and qualitative research. She has presented her research both nationally and internationally and has provided workshops on consensual qualitative research at both U.S. and international venues.

She currently serves as coeditor-in-chief of *Counselling Psychology Quarterly* and is also on the publication board of Division 29 (Society for the Advancement of Psychotherapy) of the American Psychological Association. Dr. Knox is a fellow of Division 17 (Society of Counseling Psychology) and Division 29 of the American Psychological Association.